PATCHWORK MEMORIES

PATCHWORK MEMORIES

BY WAYNE H. BETHAM

BOOK PUBLISHING

langbookpublishing.com

No part of this book may be reproduced, stored in a retrieval system, or transmitted by any means, electronic, mechanical, photocopying, recording, or otherwise without written permission from the author.

Copyright © Wayne H. Betham 2016. All rights reserved.

The right of Wayne H. Betham to be identified as author of the Work has been asserted by him in accordance with the New Zealand Copyright Act 1994.

Cover design by Blair McLean

National Library of New Zealand Cataloguing-in-Publication Data
Lang Book Publishing 2016

ISBN 978-0-9941292-7-7 – Paperback
eISBN 978-0-9941292-8-4 – eBook
eISBN 978-0-9941294-0-6 – ePub
eISBN 978-0-9941289-8-0 - Kindle

Published in New Zealand
A catalogue record for this book is available from the National Library of New Zealand.
Kei te pātengi raraunga o Te Puna Mātauranga o Aotearoa te whakarārangi o tēnei pukapuka.

INTRODUCTION

Life is like a patchwork quilt with each square telling a different story, but the entirety making a compilation of one's life. I have randomly selected different periods of my life that I found noteworthy and attempted to accumulate them into a fragment of my imagination. I have included stories from my childhood through adult and by no means exhausted the well that supplied them. The quilt will be complete when the stories end and that will be at my demise. We all have a quilt we're working on, whether we know it or not. What is displayed there may have bright colors and intricate stitching or dark overtones of black. We are the authors of our quilt and someday it will be revealed in its entirety to our glory or shame, which is the ultimate question. I hope you enjoy the few segments of my quilt I am sharing with you here.

WAYNE H. BETHAM

CHAPTER ONE

It was the winter of 1972 and the resort towns located in the San Bernardino Mountains had received their fair share of snow and cold weather for this season. I was situated between the San Gorgonio mountain range to the south, and Mt. Baldy to the north, with Big Bear Lake about twenty miles north of me, as the crow flies. The Weesha Country Club was a unique collection of homes sprawled over a seventy-five acre portion of lowland. It was nestled next to the Los Angeles Creek, mostly hidden by tall Jeffery Pines and a mixture of cedars and Manzanita scrub bushes. It was a beautiful spot. It was not too crowded since we were at the end of Seven Oaks Road, and it was a good fifteen miles off the main highway that constitutes the back road to Big Bear Lake from Los Angeles. There were log houses over a hundred years old and cabins with cedar pillars in front, as well as newer, modern homes with swimming pools and pool rooms, all intermingled throughout the property.

I, being the new caretaker, handled tending the lawns and hauling the trash, keeping water to the residences flowing and also tending the apple orchard. This orchard was on the opposite side of the creek with the log cabin, where I was staying, and the barn. It painted a beautiful picture and they were paying me to keep it that way. I was thirty-four years old at the time and had a wife, Raylene, who loved this kind of life as much as I did. She was raised in a Christian summer camp in these very same mountains. Her father was the Director of Youth Activities for a large church conference stationed in town. Life was good and the challenges at the Weesha were nominal. The equipment provided to me included an ancient pickup truck necessary for my work responsibilities. It was a forest green 1957 Chevy Apache. A lot of guys I knew would have liked to have one just like it as a classic to restore and cherish; however, my association with it was on a different level. Necessity and recreation are worlds apart when relying on a vehicle needed to perform tasks which were sometimes monumental. The trip to the landfill, about a one-hour drive, was pushing its limited life to the max. The Ford tractor, used to irrigate the apple trees, was gray much like a World War II navy warship. Printed on the front emblem, emblazoned in blue enamel was "50 Year Jubilee". I think this was just about when the darn thing was constructed. Nevertheless, all things accounted for, I didn't complain; after all, who could have asked for a better job than this, living in God's country and breathing the freshest air in California?

I got this job because I had been the acting manager at a camp, seven miles up the south mountain range, called Cedar Falls. A dirt road wound up to Cedar Falls rife with cutbacks and hairpin turns. It was as though a giant bulldozer had cut this path in as a fire break. It also served as a county road for forest rangers and firefighting vehicles. Although not intended as a road for casual travel, it did cut nearly twenty minutes off the trip to the landfill and to Redlands, the closest town.

My wife and I had a horse that we were happy to keep on hand, now that we had a place compatible with doing so. Lucky was his name and he was a good horse, even though he did have some ornery traits I needed to smooth out as soon as I could get around to it. He was a gelding and "cut proud", much to my chagrin. "Cut proud" means that when he was castrated, the man doing the job didn't slide the offending scissors far enough up the connecting

CHAPTER ONE

cords of his testicles before snipping them off. As a result, the attributes of a stallion were still evident at times. He was part-Morgan and part-Quarter Horse and the mixture was a good combination. He was fast off the get-go and had enough power to keep it up for longer than most. He was an excellent looking roan and we loved to ride him when we could, which wasn't really often enough. If we went riding in a group, with other horsemen, he always had to be the lead horse. He would chamfer and strut and sidestep around, working himself into a lather, until he finally got there. I didn't mind it because he looked so spirited and alive when he did this even though I knew it was a bad habit I needed to curb.

Hugh, the manager of Weesha, was a large man in his seventies and topped with a mop of thick gray hair. He was the type of person you liked right off and I was happy he was the one I reported to. His down-home approach to all problems eased tensions immediately and problems usually evaporated with the two of us working together to overcome them. Then there were the other members, who felt they had as much say over me as Hugh did. This caused some friction, but his "aw' shucks man, don't let the small stuff rile ya, kid" attitude allowed me to take these outbreaks in stride. I made some real friends there and the young school teacher and his wife and children were always a welcome treat for me and Raylene. We didn't see them that often but we loved the weekends they could make the trip up. They owned the smallest house on the property and it was positioned at the far end of the circle drive, overlooking the grass fairway onto which the original buildings faced. Their kids were young, ranging from five to about twelve, with a seven-year-old in the middle, all girls, and all blondes. They were a happy troop and seeing them hiking and playing on the lawn was pleasant. Watching those little towheads bobbing about effortlessly gave me a feeling of wonderment.

One evening about eight o'clock the phone rang; it was Raylene's dad calling. He was in a bind and wanted to know if I would help him out. Cedar Falls was closing down for the winter and he wondered if I would like to take care of the fifteen head of horses the camp owned over the winter months. In turn, the members of the Weesha could ride and enjoy them. He would pay for the hay and I could haul the saddles and tack down, too, so everyone could partake in the trail riding if they wanted to. It sounded good to me and I told him I would pass it along to the powers that be and get back to him later. Hugh thought it was a good idea and he gave me the go-ahead to start building the corral we would need to house these mounts. The teachers, Mike and his wife Tina, were really ecstatic about the possibility that their kids could ride through the winter and at the same time learn the responsibilities involved in the care and upkeep of horses. But Mike didn't know squat about horses, so guess who the teacher in this little scenario was going to be?

Mike helped me build the corral with timber we scrounged up on the property. I managed to find a pair of post hole diggers in the barn and then the real work began in earnest. Hard work never bothered me since my dad taught his kids the value of a hard day's labor and the satisfaction of a job well done. I would get up around five-thirty each morning and after breakfast would be digging post holes just as the sun rose over Mount San Gorgonio. It became a habit for me and with at least 30 to 40 holes to dig in my spare time, I tried to knock

CHAPTER ONE

off at least a couple each morning before my regular work. I noticed that each morning a couple of coyotes would stroll across the apple orchard approximately 150 yards west of me. They would meander back and forth as if to say, "What you gonna do about it, big guy?" This kept up for a week or two until I thought, okay, enough is enough. The following morning I took my lever-action rifle with me to the job site and propped it up against the last pole I had installed. As usual, the coyotes came strolling through the apple orchard as brass as ever, so I took the rifle and aimed just over the top of the large male. At 150 yards, I figured the .44 mag cartridge would come close enough to scare the hell out of him and teach him a little respect. I aimed carefully with the rifle propped on top of the post and squeezed off a round. To my surprise, the poor coyote jumped straight up in the air about two feet and plopped right down where he was, dead. I was trying to scare it but scared myself by killing the poor thing with a fatal shot through the heart. I buried the coyote next to the orchard and marked his grave with a mound of rocks. I felt terrible about the whole affair and to this day regret the killing of the beautiful animal. He was in a full winter coat and was a magnificent reddish orange in color. I never saw the other one again.

The day finally came when we needed to transport the herd of horses down from Cedar Falls to their new winter corral east of the orchard, behind my home in Weesha. I saddled Lucky and headed up the mountain through the back trail across the stream and into the woods. The trail wound through the big pines and finally ended up at the pipe corral at Cedar Falls, where the horses were waiting

Now camp horses are a breed apart. They are usually old and accustomed to being mistreated by several hundred kids of all ages. They don't have any spirit left in them and they know the trails better than the guides that lead them. They don't run or hardly trot at a pace faster than a slow plod. All the beatings, pleadings, or threats couldn't get them to change their modus operandi and they knew where "home" was from any section of the mountain south of Big Bear and north of Redlands. "Barn sour" is a term used to characterize these critters and it means they head for the barn when they get tired, or hungry, or just have a notion to.

I figured the easiest way to get them down was to tie each of them together by their halters and lead them down as a group. It was no simple task and after many hours of dragging, shouting, whistling and prodding I managed to get them into the corral just around sundown. Lucky was completely fagged out and so was I, and it wasn't with much resistance I called it quits for the night, washed up and went in for dinner. I left Lucky in the barn, unsaddled and tied in a stall, and the others in their new home, the corral. It was getting cold and there were still patches of snow here and there on the ground that refused to melt even though we had had several days of bright sunshine. Raylene had fixed an excellent supper for us and it wasn't too long before I headed for the bedroom to crawl under the warm covers and pass out.

It seemed like a split second since my head hit the pillow when I was awakened by the herd of horses galloping past my bedroom window at a thunderous pace. I didn't know anything that could get these nags running at this speed, especially after the hard day's ride we just completed. It didn't occur to me that the black bears that frequent the apple orchard each night would spook them

CHAPTER ONE

this much. Apparently, they did. It was around two o'clock in the morning and cold as the proverbial diggers butt. I would much rather stay in bed and let the darn things fend for themselves, but I felt responsible for their safety so I sprang out of bed, dressed and flew out to the barn. I was so thankful I had left Lucky in the stall. I can only guess Lucky wasn't as grateful as I was. Just as the saddle hit his back, I could hear the horses breaking through my split-rail fence around my log cabin and the whole mess of them blazing up the dirt road and stampeding toward Cedar Falls. I swung onto Lucky's back and swirled around in the barn, shot out the double doors and started a journey I can only describe as bizarre and scary.

Lucky took to the challenge as usual and was determined to get to the front of this mass exodus come hell or high water. As we crossed the bridge over the Los Angeles creek, I could barely see the rear horses as they reached the first switchback fifty yards ahead. I thank God to this day that it was a full moon that night so I could see, and the eerie shadows it cast over the dirt road only added to the surreal situation I found myself in.

We were at full throttle, hell-bent-for-leather, and I grabbed the saddle horn and held on for dear life. The snow patches we flew over were almost iridescent in the bright moonlight and the needle nose turns on the road almost pitch black between the high banks pushed up on either side. I could hear the horses up ahead in the cold night air with an occasional whinny floating back as if teasing poor Lucky to catch up. He did. We reached the first switchback in no time at all. Lucky planted his foreleg at the precise time to negotiate the turn, smack dab, on a frozen snow patch. His hoof splayed out from under him and we hit the ground with his belly, and slid sideways until he regained his footing. He popped up like a jack-in-the-box on steroids and flogged on once again. I stayed on, thank goodness, and was only glad he didn't roll over, ass over tea kettle and crush me, but he didn't. We were slowly gaining on them and each juncture we hit played out the same belly-sliding, hoof-scrambling melee as before.

It got to the stage where I wished I had a camera to film this scene because no one would believe it if told as it actually happened. Mile after mile we galloped, and I could feel him tiring between my legs. We finally mingled with the stragglers and slowly pulled up toward the front of the pack. It was only another half-mile to the "infamous" barn they were headed for and weaving through the cabins and tennis courts, bathrooms and cedar trees, we eventually reached their goal. The corral was still open from this morning when I picked them up, and they all scrambled inside and abruptly stopped. I slammed the gate shut and latched it. Lucky looked like a steam locomotive. He shot out white "steam" with each breath. His sides were heaving in and out and I could tell he was all in. I remember at that moment a coyote howling into the cold night air. I think it must have been the mate having the last laugh at the Mr. Toads wild ride that fateful night. I kicked Lucky's flanks and we headed back down the hill to home, a lot easier trip than the last one up. The camp horses would be okay corralled in their home court for the night and I would pick them up later, a lot later. We picked our way back down the mountain and Lucky began to settle down a bit. The sight was eerily quiet in contrast to the trip up, but we managed to find our way home safely. I put Lucky up for the night once more. I dried him off and rubbed him down and gave him a few more oats for his extraordinary performance.

CHAPTER ONE

I crawled in through the back door and said to Raylene who was waiting anxiously in the kitchen, "Too bad we don't have two horses honey; you would have enjoyed the trip."

CHAPTER 2

I was still in high school in 1963 and attending Newbury Park Academy, located in Southern California somewhere between Camarillo and Simi Valley. This was a boarding school and my roommate was a great guy named Jim Lynn. Jim was raised on an orange orchard, deep in the heart of orange country. The town's name was Santa Paula and at that time, a sleepy little place you would miss if not paying attention driving through it. Jim's dad was the manager of the ranch and was also a reserve cop from Santa Paula. They had a small California bungalow-type home and adjoining their barn was a water tower, a diesel tank, and a tool shed. I remember the soil as being sandy and fine, the kind that permeates everything. We were always dusty and dirty to some degree.

It was summer time and I was staying with Jim for a few days on the ranch. We slept in the barn and did just about anything we pleased. Life was good. We decided to ride a couple of horses into town to the local Dairy Queen and each get a root beer float. The only trouble was we had no horses. Jim's dad said he had a friend, Matthew, that owned a few working horses that we might borrow to make our trip. After a short phone call, we had secured a couple for the job. Now, these were "working" horses - not barn-soured and spoiled equestrians we were accustomed to. They were used almost daily for rounding up cattle and occasionally performed in the local rodeos. We eagerly hiked the mile or two to where the horses were. Matthew was waiting for us when we arrived and had saddled them for us already. Then after some cautioning, he wished us a fun journey. He said these mares were quarter horses and used to cutting cattle so they were sensitive to the bit and quick off the start.

We politely thanked him and climbed aboard. I could tell mine was fresh and ready to go and so was Jim's. We trotted for a bit and when out of sight of Matthew, dug our heels in their flanks and let them rip. I was smart enough to have grabbed a handful of mane because if I hadn't, I would have been sitting in mid-air watching the horse's rear end flying down the middle of a row of orange trees. We were running neck-n-neck and enjoying the cold air blowing in our faces. Man, this was living. All the emotions of primeval man were oozing throughout our beings. We were Hopalong Cassidy and Red Ryder chasing the bandits, or whatever, and we were gaining.

The orange trees were flying by and becoming just a blur on both sides; the brim of my hat was flapping up and down depending on how I cocked my head. Jim was laughing out loud and he did that on various occasions, either when he was having fun or when he was scared stiff. I didn't have to think long to realize which one it was now. I looked back to see how he was when I made a serious mistake. Remember, these were working horses and sensitive to the bit. I inadvertently tweaked the reins to the right and my mare, "Hellfire", assumed I wanted to go right. You know there isn't much room between orange trees when you enter the rows from the side. Hellfire didn't think about that and figured I knew what the hell I was doing. I didn't. I did not know a quarter horse could turn on a dime at full tilt and give you eight cents change. They can, and this one did. Did you know orange trees have nasty spikes on them? I found out the hard way. Fortunately, Jim's horse didn't follow, so after the deserved heckling, he chased mine down and brought her back for me.

CHAPTER 2

I would like to say the rest of the trip was uneventful, but it wasn't. Having the wind sufficiently knocked out of me, I wasn't in too good a mood to be nice, especially to horses named "Hellfire". I got back in the saddle and once again we were off. I waited, however, until we got clear of the orange trees before we cut 'em loose this time. Once again everything was good. Hell, more than good, things were great. Once again my cowboy hat was flappin' up and down so I pushed the crazy thing up on my forehead and became a carbon copy of Gabby Hayes rippin' down the dirt road chasin' Roy. Jim was having a blast too, and we were both enrapt at the moment. Unfortunately, the dirt road was fast disappearing and a two-lane highway was dead ahead. I appropriately used the words "dead ahead" because if we couldn't stop these critters, that's what we would be. I hauled back on the reins as hard as I could and put Hellfire into a slide. It's a different feeling sitting atop a speeding horse and not having the legs working down there. She was sitting on her haunches and we were still cruising. Did I mention these were working horses? Not only can the horses turn on a dime and give you eight cents change, but they are also quick on the git-go and easy on the bit. But Matthew failed to mention they can stop on a nickel and give you four cents change. Trouble was, I could only stop on a dime with no cents change. I remember how surreal it was as I flew over Hellfire's head with my hat cocked back looking down into her eyes from above. She looking back at me with a "What the hell are you doing?" look in her eyes. I wish I knew. Jim was laughing like crazy and it wasn't the "scared stiff" laugh either. I did mention the dirt around them parts was fine and dusty, and when the dust cleared, I looked like Al Jolson doing blackface vaudeville except with Gabby Hayes's hat. One of the reasons we were riding to town beside the Root Beer float was to pick up some chicks. Nothin' cooler than riding a horse into town, right? Well, I looked like hell, and any prospects of hitting it off with the ladies went right round the bend. But wait a minute. Things weren't a total loss. I remembered we had to cross a river before we hit town and while swimming the horses over I could wash myself off at the same time. Brilliant; like my daddy said, necessity was the mother of invention. Ha, ha, this "invention" was about to backfire on me big time. I was lying on my back, wondering how the heck I got here. I was six-foot, two-inches tall, weighed 220 pounds and was tough as nails. Hellfire was a mare weighing around 1500 pounds, standing about fourteen-hands high and was tougher than old boot leather. I think I had met my match and it was time to ease into this relationship a little at a time. After Jim had quit laughing, the horses were settled down. My back said it was still part of my anatomy and I sat up on the ground and dusted my pride off as well as the rest of myself. I said, "Well, Jim, this is one hell of a start; I've been bucked off twice in ten miles." He wasn't too sympathetic, more "better you than me" kind of thing. I remounted, and we rode on a lot slower than before, mainly because we were paralleling the main highway, and I didn't want any foul-ups anywhere close to automobiles and trucks. We got an occasional "toot" and whistles from the passing motorists, but all done in fun. Things were good again, and now it was just Jim and Wayne riding to town to get a root beer float each, and maybe a sweet senorita.

From South Mountain Road, we had to cross a large bridge into Santa Paula. This bridge spanned the river flowing behind Jim's ranch and into the Ventura City limits. It was about 100 yards wide and slow moving and deep. I figured the bridge being too dangerous

CHAPTER 2

to walk across; it would be better to swim the beasts over and before you could say Bobs your uncle, we'd be there. There was nothing to it. We traversed past the bridge and found ourselves standing at the river's edge. Being close up to the water, I began realizing this wasn't going to be an easy thing to do after all. I knew horses could swim instinctively, but I wasn't worried about the horses; it was a little closer to home, I was worried for me. I got off Hellfire and tightened up the cinch on the saddle a bit just to be sure I wasn't going to be floating downstream with just a saddle between my legs. Jim did the same, and pretty soon we were ready to take the plunge. I couldn't have used a more apropos term, for before you knew it we were off. I jabbed my boot heels into old Hellfire's flanks once again, and we shot out into the river just like a working horse is supposed to do. I am used to riding camp horses and forgot to grab a hunk of the mane just before the "jab" part. Thank God, though that I did manage to latch onto the saddle horn; otherwise, it would have been the ass over tea kettle or more truthfully, tea kettle over ass. Hellfire started in, swimming just like a pro. I hung on and stayed in the saddle until I could tell it was difficult for the poor horse to keep her head above water, let alone mine too. It was difficult to continue swimming that way for such a long distance. I slid out of the saddle and just hung on to the saddle horn, trying to keep my feet free of the thrashing hooves below. The water was cool and inviting on such a hot summer afternoon, and I would have stripped down to nothing if I weren't in the middle of civilization. My boots got sucked off by the current, and my wish would've almost come true if I hadn't a sturdy belt around my waist. We were nearing the opposite shore, and I started searching for a place to land. Yes, I had washed the dust off my face and everywhere else too and was ready for the D.Q. Trouble was, there wasn't a decent place to put into shore. The banks were covered with willow shoots and scrub brush, and I began to wish God had put fingers by horse's hooves so we could pull ourselves out of this mess. All the time we were floating farther west and the town was getting further away. I didn't know where Jim was but could hear him laughing in the distance. Which "laugh" was anybody's guess. Finally, Hellfire found her footing on a sand bar, she gained her balance and we walked out onto the waiting shore. A few minutes later Jim came in the same way, and we found ourselves under a shady tree on the opposing bank together. Water was gushing out of his boots, and my socks were half off which made me look like I had Aladdin's shoes on. Everything we had was soaked through, but we didn't care; we had met the challenge and won. I must have looked a sight riding bootless on Hellfire and weather-beaten to boot. Not the suave cowboy looking for a date and a root beer float in town at the local D.Q.

There was one singular thought that remained silent and unspoken: we still had to go back the same way we came. Oh well, we mounted up and rode into town slow and easy and with a little more distance to traverse than planned. The distance was alright though, since we had to dry out some before we got there. The D.Q was in the distance, and it wasn't long before we were fishing through our wet wallets for a buck or two to pay for those luscious root beer floats. With the mares tied to a tree by the parking lot and the root beer floats still lingering in our throats, I lay on top of the picnic table outside the Dairy Queen. I said, "You know, Jim, I think it would be okay to lead the horses across the bridge. Do you reckon?"

CHAPTER 2

"Just thinking the same thing," he replied. Any thoughts of luscious blondes or gorgeous brunettes quickly faded from view halfway across the river and would have to wait for some other day. Life was good again, and we were reveling in it.

CHAPTER 3

Norman Butterbread was a half breed, his mother being a full-blooded Indian and his dad a hard-headed German. He got the best and worst traits from both of them. He was arrested and jailed for rustling cattle and stubborn as hell about his right to do so. I met him through a mutual friend of mine while dabbling in the mining business. I was up in the Chocolate Mountains, just south of Lake Isabella, east of Bakersfield, California. There was an old deserted tungsten mine there that hadn't been in operation since the second world war. I was up there in the early 1970's with Dick McGavock, my construction foreman from the White Memorial Hospital in Los Angeles, California. I was Director of Maintenance and Engineering there, and we spent a lot of time spinning yarns about various quests we wanted to do and this led me here. Men are boys with bigger toys and bank accounts. There was a mine up in the mountains, Norman said, and he would show us where it was. We were to meet him at Bodfish Restaurant right next to the lake on Sunday morning, and we could head out right after we ate together. I agreed, and we met on the appointed day.

Norman had a young wife and baby who accompanied him for breakfast. They were obviously destitute, and this is why he resorted to rustling, to feed his family. I liked him right off and didn't judge him for the radical methods he used to provide for his family. He knew the mountains and the more I got to know him, the more I realized he was like his mother. He had the instincts of an Indian in the mountains and I found that reassuring. Little did I realize how much I would be relying on them at that time.

I told Norman I was treating breakfast, so order whatever they wanted. He was surprised and exclaimed, "Hey, thanks a million." He was about twenty-one or two years old and his wife no more than sixteen or so, beautiful and very naive, and dressed in a simple dress and sweater. She had no makeup on, and I doubt she had ever used any in her entire life. Her hair was combed and neat, but her humble background was all too evident. She was shy and blushed all the time when attention turned to her. The waitress came and I ordered eggs over medium and hash browns, sourdough toast and coffee. Next, the wife whispered to her husband if she could get a steak. Overhearing her comment, I said sure, whatever you want. She wiggled back in her seat with a big grin on her face and she said, "I want a steak."

The waitress said, "How do you want it?"

Now this shook her up a bit, and I could see the red starting to glow around her neck region. "Uh," she said, and then remembered my egg order and said emphatically, "Over medium."

The waitress tried to stifle a laugh and said, "Honey, you get it rare, medium or well done. Over medium is for eggs, not a steak."

The poor girl would have crawled under the table if she could. The red turned bright crimson, and she slumped into her seat, totally embarrassed. I jumped in and tried to rescue the situation and told the waitress, "If she wants it over medium give it to her that way. Medium sounds good to me."

"Okay, what sides do you want?" she asked. "We have hash browns, country potatoes, biscuits and gravy or grits." This barrage of questions was more than the poor girl could endure. My heart sank, I wish I could have done something to rectify the situation, but it was way past that time. I almost saw a tear welling

CHAPTER 3

up in her right eye and thought this had gone far enough. "Let's make it a steak, medium, hash browns sourdough toast and how about a large milk and some cream o' wheat for the baby?" I could see a ton weight fall off the shoulders of Norm's young wife, and we settled in for a hearty breakfast.

The road up to the mine was overgrown and rocky since it hadn't seen a grader or dozer since the second world war. We parked at the base of the hill and hiked to the mine entrance about a mile from the road. We had to scramble over sections of the road that had washed out over the years. We finally reached a spot where large timbers stuck out of the ground, holding a winch to retrieve the ore carts up the shaft from the mine itself. This spot was a pit mine, and the tunnel sank into the mountainside at a thirty-degree angle. The entrance was passable but covered. I had brought a black light to assess the ore content in the mine, and it also had a regular light to guide us. Dick was up in years and overweight, so he opted to wait at the entrance while Norm and I slid into the mine to see what survey the area. I was leery of rattlesnakes and scorpions so played it cautious from the start. We snaked our way down about 50 yards and took a breather. The sides had collapsed in a lot of places, but we managed to get down to the large opening which was like an area for storage or lunch breaks. There is nothing blacker than a mine shaft. If I turned out the light, I wouldn't be able to see my hand an inch from my face. If I didn't consciously open and shut my eyelids, I never would have known if they were open or closed. We worked our way down to a lower level where the digging had stopped so many years ago. I turned off the light and turned on the black light. I wasn't prepared for the incredible sight that lay before us. Tungsten ore shines like star lights, and the entire shaft was lit like a starry night in winter in the middle of the desert. It was magnificent. The sparkling light engulfed us and felt as if we were floating in space since the lamps shone from beneath us as well as from around us. I could only surmise why the mine shut down, and it wasn't from lack of ore. The prices must have tumbled after the war was over, and it wasn't profitable to continue mining. However, today the price was back up, and I wanted to see what I could do to restart the production.

We made our way to the surface and I told Dick what we had found. We all were excited at the possibilities awaiting us. We spent several weeks trying to find the owner of the property where the mine was, only to continually hit brick walls with no answers as to his whereabouts. We finally gave up the search and chalked it up to a bad deal.

Norm said he knew of another possibility up on top of the mountain that showed promise. It was a yellow outcropping of rocks that looked like sulfur but didn't have the pungent odor associated with this ore when lit with a match. It might be uranium, he said, since this is a yellow ore and who knows what it is unless we checked it out. He said he could get a couple of mountain-bred horses, and we could check it out for ourselves later. He brought the two horses over to the Wishing Well Motel where I was staying the following morning. They were hitched up to his pick-up and upon seeing them in the beat-up horse trailer, figured we were in for some fun. I couldn't tell what the horses looked like while loaded, but thought Norm knew them, and that was good enough for me.

CHAPTER 3

We drove down some winding dirt roads till we arrived at a large open meadow at the base of the mountain. Norm dropped the loading gate to the trailer and backed the two ponies out and hitched them to the side of the trailer. My heart sank as I saw these scrawny beasts tied there. Apparently he could see my disappointment and said, "Don't be fooled by their size and shape, these ponies are truly mountain bred and know what they are doing."

I replied, "I sure hope so." He saddled them up, I swung aboard the bigger of the two and was when surprised my feet didn't hit the ground on either side. We tied the saddlebags on with a canteen of water, the Geiger counter I borrowed from the emergency kit at the hospital and some food and off we went. There wasn't any trail to follow, so we made our own as we headed straight up the mountain side.

It was early in the morning, just after the sun up; I would say sixish or so and the air was fresh and inviting. The smell of old leather and the sweat laden horse blankets was a familiar bouquet to the nostrils and not unpleasant in any way. The pine trees and rock outcroppings were plentiful and we soon began the tedious switchbacking back and forth to gain the altitude we wanted. Norm knew the way and I just followed behind. Conversation ceased and soon the only sounds I heard were the creaking of the leather saddles and the occasional snort of the horses. I also heard the plod, plod, plod of the horses' hooves as we sought the best way up. By ten o'clock we managed to reach a small mesa atop a foothill and we dismounted to give the horses a rest. We had been traversing for four solid hours and my butt was tired. I was beginning to understand what Norm was trying to tell me about "mountain" horses. They didn't show their tiredness in any way and my admiration of them was beginning to blossom. After a few sips of water and some small talk we were back in the saddle and again attacking the hillside to gain the summit.

By noon, we had reached the last leg, prior to attaining our goal, and the trees were thinning out exposing the rock and shale crags protruding from the mountain slopes. My rear end was getting sore now, and I was convinced the ponies were feeling the strain also. Upon reaching the top, we spent another hour trying to find the yellow deposits and hopefully some uranium ore. Our food was gone and the water was getting thin also. We passed some natural springs where the horses drank but it wasn't clean enough for me to fill the canteens. I asked Norm if he was hungry yet, and he replied, "You want something to eat?" I said it would be nice. He said, "Okay, let's head over to that pine tree over there."

"Why that pine?" I asked?

"Because that's the only one around here with pine nuts," he said. We dismounted once more and began foraging under the pine for the precious nuts. There were thousands of them, and I looked in the saddle bags for a sack to fill. I love the taste of pine nuts and would have ridden right by them if it weren't for my Indian guide who knew the mountains and what to look for. He said only some particular trees have the edible nuts, you have to know what to look for and he was right. We filled a large sack to bring back with us and again began our hunt for the elusive ore.

I wasn't too crazy about remounting the ponies but had no other choice at the moment. My rear end was telling me enough, but my pride told me to shut up. The squeaking saddles and smelly blankets had lost some of their charms but still I knew we had to continue on. Norm said we were getting close and I only hoped

CHAPTER 3

he was right. Sure enough, it wasn't but a short time and we were there. He was right; there was a substantial amount of yellow ore rising right out of the ground. It looked unnatural the way it stood out from its surroundings.

I quickly dismounted and dug the Geiger counter out of the saddle bag. I switched it on and ran the wand over the outcropping, nothing. I tested the readings with the luminous dial of my wrist watch, and the counter went wild. I waved it over the ore again and nothing. Dead silence. I tried several sites to no avail. I know we discovered a large load of mysterious rocks or some other unusual mineral, but it wasn't uranium. Hell, what did I know anyway? I sure wasn't a geologist, that's for sure. Disappointment stemming from both of us flooded our countenance, and the effort put out to get here took its toll on us, but we shrugged it off and started down. I should have gotten some samples but was so tired it never occurred to me.

By now it was getting late in the afternoon, and the shadows were lengthening quickly. We had a fair way to go and two tired horses to get there on. I told Norm so, and he said, "Hell no, these ponies got a lot of spunk left in 'em yet." He said he knew a shortcut down the mountain; it was steeper but going down was easier so it should be okay. Little did I realize how wrong those words would play out. It was dark now, and the scene from the tungsten mine came into my mind's eye. We started to cross a massive rock slide that rose above us and fell to infinity below us. The horses walked on as if it was no big thing to them, but I had other feelings roiling around in both my head and gut. Each step of the horses produced bright sparks flying off their iron shoes. The rocks were flint laden, and the results were surprising. I had never seen anything like it before in my life and I would never again. The show went on for some time until we crossed completely over the slide. I swung over to one side and watched the fireworks shooting out from eight hooves each creating a spectacle of their own and each as amazing as the next.

We ambled into a dry river bed and followed it down, down, down. Norm stopped and I asked what the problem was. He said there was a drop off dead ahead and we had to backtrack to get around it. We transversed the ravine and worked our way down past the dry waterfall. I looked back as we resumed the gully's trail and shone my flashlight on to a dry waterfall about three stories high. If we had gone on another few feet, we would have dropped about thirty feet down onto the rocks below. How Norm saw this in the pitch dark, I will never know. The horses probably did and refused to go further themselves.

After the third or fourth "waterfall", I suggested we strip the ponies down and sleep in the dry waterbed and continue in the morning when we could see better. I was played out and I figured the ponies were too. He said we were getting close to reaching the base and that we should push on. Several more dry drops were routed around and passed as we worked our way down to the foothills where the truck and trailer were waiting below. The terrain started to even out and the incline became less acute.

I began to relax a bit from the harrowing mountain crevice we had just negotiated for the past several hours. It wasn't but a few minutes after we walked out from the base of the hill that the moon arose right over the opposing mountain range. It wasn't a regular moon either, but a huge harvest moon as big as a giant pizza peeking over the valley below. It cast its eerie light over the

CHAPTER 3

whole scene before us. I could see the truck and trailer about a mile down the valley floor. There was a huge natural meadow before us, and with the pine trees behind us and this before us, I felt a hard ride and a place of rest.

I said to Norm that these nags were finished. He said, "Hell no, they still got life in 'em, watch." He planted his heels in his pony's' sides and yelled, "Giddyup." The "dead" horse leaped forward as if it had been stuck in the ass with a ten thousand volt cattle prod. Mine wasn't about to be outdone and followed suit. We raced full tilt down the valley floor in the faint glow of the moon. After loading the ponies in the trailer and driving down the dirt road to the restaurant in Bodfish, we settled into the comfort of a padded booth and ordered a steak dinner. Norm, looked up at me with a wry grin on his face and drawled, "'Ain't this better than sleepin' on a stinkin' saddle blanket in a cold ravine somewhere up there in the mountains?" You know, he was dead right.

CHAPTER 4

Senior year in high school is one of the best and worst of the four needed to graduate. In the senior year, you have finally found the friends you are comfortable with and realize time is running out. If you are going to make the most of the year, you had better do it now or forever miss this golden opportunity. Living in the boys' dormitory at my boarding high school in Newbury Park, California was a culture shock in and of itself.

Living away from home for the first time in my life opened up a new and exciting world full of opportunities for mischief and adventure. I had gone through several roommates over the first three years due to various reasons. The first was a science nut who I found pacing back and forth at the foot of my bed at two o'clock in the morning mumbling his scientific equations and chemical compounds with his 3x5 cards and horned rim glasses. I don't know if this guy ever slept, but I knew if I wanted to, he would have to go. The next was a sports junkie who thought all the clothes in the room belonged to him. He had no compulsion against using my underwear or socks anytime he saw fit. Now I have various kinds of clothes. There are my good clothes I wear to church. There are my school clothes I wear to class. There are my old clothes I wear to work, etc., etc. Wayne Thompson wore my good socks to play baseball in or a nice school shirt to play football in.

He had another attribute that finally broke the proverbial camel's back. It's hard to put into words, but I will give it a try. Between each dorm room was a bathroom consisting of a toilet and shower we shared with our neighbor. Wayne was constantly plugging up the toilet with every use. This got to be a chronic problem and his reputation began to spread throughout the boys' dorm. I finally threatened him with certain death if he ever got ours clogged again. Naturally he never claimed responsibility and he was an expert at sneaking out after his dastardly deed. He finally got my hint and started visiting other rooms whenever nature called and slipped effortlessly out the side door of the newest victims' room through the opposing room's door. He found this easy since there were two doors to every bathroom.

On one occasion, his sneaky ritual (pardon the pun) backfired. Jim, my future roommate and I were visiting with Johnny Crawford, our friend down the hall. Johnny, mid-sentence, stopped and as if struck by lightning, yelled, "Thompson, is that you in there?" A loud giggle emitted from the closed bathroom door as Wayne hurriedly ejected himself through the opposite side door. Johnny jumped up and ran to the bathroom and slung open the door. The verbal abuses he yelled out after Thompson were echoing down the hall as he retrieved a fork someone had left on the window sill and stabbed the offending mass in the toilet. He began chasing Thompson down the hall with it. The hallways had linoleum floors and the walls were painted with a high gloss light green paint. There were only two sources of light coming in through two glass doors leading out to the fire escapes at both ends of the hall. The picture of Thompson's silhouette running for his life toward the east entrance still brings a smile to my face as Johnny, upon reaching the fire escape, flung the brandished culprit at Wayne who by this time was fleeing across the side lawn and up the chapel steps next door. Luckily it missed its target but Wayne never forgot his close call with nature that fateful day, you might say of his own making.

CHAPTER 4

Jim moved in soon after the Crawford incident and we remained roommates till he left in his junior year.

This boarding school was a Christian-run academy that believed young men should not only be schooled in the finer arts of medicine, law, and business, but taught a rudimentary understanding of the blue collar aspects of life too. Jim and I fell in the blue collar points and were quickly introduced to the farming and auto mechanical trades of what the school offered. Jim was assigned to the farm shop and handled the growing of crops and I was the new auto mechanic who fixed cars after classes each day. Being a farmer at this young age was a responsibility Jim took very seriously. He used to rise early in the morning about five am, head down to the farm shop and fire up the little Cat. He would hook on the disc or plow or other implement and drag the darn thing back and forth across the field right in front of the girl's dorm. Jim loved to sing and he did on most occasions as he worked away just prior to the sun up each day. The trouble was Jim couldn't carry a tune in a bucket and his songs, mostly Homer 'n' Jethro ballads or Ray Stevens' songs, split the morning air like a dull knife. Funny though, he knew all the words and never just sang the first stanzas. I would accompany him regularly and stand on the rear shackles of the Cat. As we farmed the corn fields, we sang duets together. It wasn't long before we read in the school newspaper about the horrible serenading coming from the farmers as they worked in the fields. They mentioned how the crops would probably fail and the farm animals die from the intense cruelty inflicted on them each day. This attention did little to dampen Jim's spirits and the "abuse" continued throughout the school year.

Directly across from the farm shop, which was just an old

barn standing there for at least eighty years or more, was the egg ranch. The school prided themselves in their veggie eggs and sold thousands of them each day to health shops and supermarkets all over the Southland. I never quite knew what a "veggie" egg was and concluded that it must be that the chickens were fed only vegetable products and no meat.

Down the dirt road from the farm shop and egg ranch was the dairy where they kept thirty or forty head of Holsteins the kids milked every day. This was a handy arrangement that kept Jim and I happy whenever we got hungry and needed food. Tom was the dairy manager and a good friend of ours, so getting milk was no problem any time we wanted. The eggs were there for the taking since the chickens were in wire cages lined up by rows and standing row by row for at least a half mile.

The farm shop had a large forge, never used now but operational, and it made a fantastic platform for our private stove. We had a sheet of clean steel we set over the coals and soon scrambled eggs were on the fire and the feeding begun. Salt was available too since sacks of it were stacked in the barn for the water softeners in the laundry. Grinding some rock salt down to shaker size was no problem. Life was good and on some chilly nights this ritual actually took the sting off the nose and fingers after a cold morning of farming.

It was while gouging ourselves in the barn we came up with the bright idea of repainting the barn's roof. As I mentioned, this structure was erected many years ago before the school owned it and painted on the roof was the famous advertisement in its day, "Mail Pouch Tobacco". The school was quite happy the paint was faded and almost unreadable, so we figured it our civic duty to rectify the situation. This was one occasion in which Wayne Thompson was

CHAPTER 4

also involved, and it was with no little trepidation he climbed the ladder to the top of the barn. He complained incessantly about the danger involved and shook noticeably from sheer terror the higher we climbed. We had scrounged up a few gallons of white, pink and beige paint that we mixed together in a five-gallon bucket to do the job. Jim and I were to paint the words "Mail" and "Pouch" and Wayne was to do the "Tobacco". We decided to do this at night so our deed would go unnoticed until the following morning. The barn was located across the highway from the school itself and since the school was situated on a steep rise about a hundred yards from the road, the view was exceptionally good. We worked most of the night and with no moon to light the way it got a little dicey fifty feet off the ground with no safety equipment. We quickly descended off the roof and cleaned up the mess as best we could before heading for mandatory worship service held each morning before classes.

The vice principle had the morning service and before he got into his thought for the day he reflected on the new paint job on the barn roof. He expounded on the selflessness of the volunteers who so eagerly donated their time to such a task but denounced the disservice afforded the school's reputation as an institution of higher learning, because whoever did it couldn't spell "Tobacco": it was incorrectly spelled T-o-b-b-a-c-o. The shame produced from such a thoughtless act was humiliating for the school authorities. Thompson, you maniac, I said, how could you be so brainless? Wayne just replied that while he was filling in the old letters he lost sight of some of the outlines in the dark and it came out wrong. He said he was too scared of falling off the roof to really care how it was spelled.

The minister of the church had two sons that used to attend the academy but now were employed in the broom factory, another student-operated cash cow for the school. They were constantly getting into some kind of situation that bordered on trouble; not serious enough for any discipline, but definitely caused some frowns from the administration.

The newest project was right up my alley, a sand dune buggy. Now this sand buggy wasn't just a ride-around-the-dune type vehicle; it was a stompin', screaming drag machine. A few miles up the coast was Pismo Beach, where such activities were conducted. We fashioned a frame from box metal scrounged up around the school and welded it together in the farm shop. The engine was a Hemi Chrysler, 392 cubic inches of raw muscle. We needed a transmission that could handle the horsepower, so got a Cadillac LaSalle three-speed manual transmission and adapted it to the Chrysler. We didn't have enough cash left to buy the shifting mechanism, so during the tryouts just stuck it in second gear and zoomed around the school campus in that one gear. We came across some zoomies (exhaust manifolds) that are the kind that just stick straight out from the engine and blow blue flames a foot or so out the ends whenever you goose it hard.

We used to cruise over Jim's fields trying to see how it might handle in the dirt (the closest thing to sand in our situation). Even stuck in the second gear we were always blowing up the rear end, either twisting off an axle or stripping the gears. I said we should go down to the wrecking yard in Thousand Oaks and pick up a Buick Roadmaster rear end. After some adjustments to the frame to accept the coil spring set up verses the leaf spring type, we were ready to rip. We hadn't installed a proper gas tank yet so

CHAPTER 4

were using a large coffee can taped to the frame to just get the feel of how it would perform. The guys worked a month to get enough cash to buy a new model carburetor just on the market for a high output Cadillac engine. It was the type E Carter AFB and it was worth the wait and the money. We filled the coffee can with gas and fired her up. You could hear it over the whole school. The zoomies were zooming and the engine was roaring and we all jumped on board and headed out to the closest field. The coffee can was good for about 2 to 3 minutes of fun and then it was refill time. We were shooting huge rooster tails in the air with our rear tires and blue flames out both sides as we tore up the countryside yelling and screaming with pure joy. You'd really can't put into words the feeling of freedom and wonderment, excitement and fear, all rolled up into one ecstatic moment in time. You think our creation and Dr. Frankenstein's had nothing in common, but what we had just created put his in the crapper. Our cheeks were flushed and the dirt flying around us covered our faces but none of this mattered, we were in the state of complete ecstasy. Patow, patow, burrr, burrr, kachink, kachink, whaaaa. Outta' gas. We sat there in total silence for a second or two before we yelled in unison either because we were alive or because we were excited. We scrambled off the rig and after I finagled with the shifting forks and found neutral, started pushing it back to the farm shop to finish working on it. I was still trembling from the test run and said to the guys to let me make one last run before we tear it apart to fit the tank, etc. They agreed so we filled her up, which took all of ten seconds, and fired her up once more. We jumped on board and headed straight up the double drive towards the administration building where I revved it up and popped the clutch. We had attracted quite a crowd, and the wheelie I popped accentuated the mood with a couple of skid marks snaking across the parking lot. We careened around the boy's dorm and promptly ran out of gas and coasted to a halt atop the rise the road made prior to entering the faculty housing area.

It wasn't two minutes before the principal pulled up behind us and jumped out of his car screaming about what sort of nincompoops we were for endangering student's lives by such rash behavior and such. It took him several moments before he could continue as he had trouble catching his breath. Since I was driving he aimed his fury directly at me, and that suited the other guys just fine. "Be in my office in half an hour," he said emphatically and stormed off. We pushed the buggy back to the shop in silence and finally I said, "Well, I might as well get it over with," and headed for the appointment.

I knocked on his office's door frame and waited for him to flag me in with his hand. He stated that he should eject me from the school altogether but since it was approaching six weeks leave time when all the kids go home for a long weekend, he would be lenient with me and give me some free labor to do instead of expulsion. Now this form of punishment was common to boarding schools where one works off the offense by doing some sort of work to recompense the infraction. He took me up to the swimming pool and showed me at least a half acre of weeds that he wanted to be pulled prior to me going home for the weekend. He knew it was at least a week's worth of labor there and smirked as he left. "Oh," he said in parting, "if you get it done in the time you can go home for whatever is left of the weekend." This was Thursday afternoon and no way was I going home.

CHAPTER 4

I lay in bed that night and wondered what I could do to finish the job prior to Friday afternoon when everyone would leave. Jim asked me what I was so quiet about and I told him my dilemma. You'll think of something, he said, as he rolled over and promptly fell asleep. I sprang out of bed around three o'clock and quietly dressed and headed to the dairy. Tom was herding the cows in for morning milking and I asked him if I could borrow the tractor and manure scoop for a couple of hours. He said fine just bring it back as soon as I finished the job. I started it up and drove to the swimming pool area where the weeds were waiting. It only took several passes with the scoop before the ground looked like it was leveled by a pro. Not a weed in sight and only five o'clock in the morning. I was surveying my excellent job when the principal walked by with his briefcase in hand. He looked at the clean field and looked at me sitting on the tractor grinning from ear to ear, he scratched his head with his free hand and shook his head and walked on without a word said. I returned the tractor to Tom and made it to breakfast and worship before class. I thanked the Lord for giving me the wherewithal to get the job done so I could go home with the rest of the kids. Driving home that weekend was just a little sweeter than most and it was some days before the smile faded from my smug face. I had met the enemy and prevailed. Life was good.

CHAPTER 5

Summer vacation was fast approaching and the guys in the dorm were talking about what jobs they were trying to line up for the summer to make some extra money. Rick Whithey was a neighbor of ours in the room directly east of us and he had worked in Alaska as a fisherman for one of the largest canneries in Anchorage. He said they provided him a boat and other necessities which they would deduct from his first haul. He said he averaged two to three thousand dollars a week and even though the work was hard, it paid off over the three months of summer. He had purchased a used Jaguar roadster, a 1960 vintage, and had paid cash for it so naturally we were all ears. Two to three thousand bucks was like a million to us greenhorns and the thought of earning it provoked a lot of thoughts. I took Rick aside and talked to him about the both of us trying it out for the summer. He said he had done it for several years in a row and he was getting tired of it and thought a stint at lumberjacking in Oregon was more in line with what he wanted to do. He said he knew a man in Roseburg that hired young high school students to set chokers for him over the summer and he paid pretty well too. I didn't know what "setting chokers" meant but figured it couldn't be too hard, and with me being fit and tough I thought I could handle anything thrown at me. The job entailed working six days a week from before sun-up to beyond sundown. It paid around three thousand a month and in 1963 that was damn good money no matter what the job. We agreed to share the costs of getting up there and for an apartment, etc. We would leave right after school was out, and after loading our stuff into Rick's little Jag roadster (no easy task), we were off.

The trip up Highway 5 was uneventful except when Rick asked me to drive so he could sleep. Now I consider myself a pretty good driver but this Jag was a different animal altogether. It had a close ratio mesh transmission and shifting it was a pain in the butt. I felt like I was operating a sewing machine with close tolerances, not a chunk of "Detroit Iron" like I was used to. It took a while until I finally got the hang of it and proceeded to our new home.

Roseburg was a quaint little town, and I liked it from the start. It didn't take long to realize the city was divided into two sections. One section was "Before the blast" and the other "After the blast". I inquired as to this "Blast" and was told a train had come through town many years back, loaded with high explosives, and somehow they had ignited and blew half the town off the face of the earth. I promptly asked if any more explosives were traversing through their town and was reassured there wasn't. We found a cute little apartment in a town called the Winchester Arms. It consisted of two two-storied bungalow type buildings and contained only ten to twelve units in the two buildings. We took a lower unit and moved our stuff in.

Rick said we needed to get outfitted so into town we went to the local hardware store. It looked as though it was built at the turn of the century and was from the pre-blast era. It was countrified with its pot-bellied stove and huge shelves lining the walls stacked with boxes of boots and clothes and some things I had never seen before. The smell was unique and not unpleasant to the senses. It was linseed oil and wax and leather and all types of ancient aromas. Rick asked the proprietor to see some "calks" and rain gear, suspenders, long sleeved work shirts and cloth gloves. I asked Rick why the cloth gloves? He said leather won't work for what we were

CHAPTER 5

going to do. Leather gloves, he went on, can't feel the wire slivers sticking out of the chokers and when you do feel them it's too late: they're already punctured through and into your finger. That was good enough for me. Calks are boots with metal studs protruding from the soles to help you from slipping off logs and such. I was getting a real education in lumberjacking right off the start and it all sounded strange and wonderful at the same time.

We drove into Glide, a little hamlet outside of Roseburg, where Dietrich Logging was stationed, and we signed up. The "crummie", a station wagon type of vehicle, would pick us up in front the Winchester Arms at 3:30 am sharp Monday morning.

Rick told me to bring a big lunch because I would need it. I watched as he filled his pail with several sandwiches and a few candy bars and in the lid, where the thermos usually was, he crammed in some Sunshine fruit pies and Oreo cookies. I said, "What the hell, are we staying for a week?"

He laughed and replied, "You'll see." I stood 6'2" tall and weighed around 280 lbs., a few pounds over my weight, but most people didn't think I was overweight, just stout. I felt I was still tough enough to do any job I had to.

High lead logging is when there is a tower erected on top of the mountain or setting, with two large wire cables stretching from the top chives to the tree line a couple of hundred yards below the cut section. The area where the trees have already been cut and sectioned off to varied lengths by the sawyers. These cables were about 2" in diameter and the lead line hung from the top of the tower to the corner holt (a pulley anchored to a sturdy tree stump) located at the far end of the field. The tail line looped through the corner holt and then through a tail block several yards over and also anchored to a stump. It then headed back up to the tower top forming a gigantic triangle. Inside this triangle is called the "bite." If you happened to be in the bite when a tailholt or corner block gave way that is what you got. On the lead line was perched two chokers made of steel cables about 5/8" diameter and about six feet apart. These chokers dangled down from the mainline about 25' to 30' long, and at the end of the choker was the bell and nubbin. This set up was referred to as the rigging. The bell was a cast steel shape that acted like a slip knot when shoved up the choker, and the nubbin, a roundish shaped steel configuration fastened to the end of the choker. It is the size of a tennis ball, it was looped around a log and inserted back into the bell, making the log ready for retrieval. Since the choker setters were operating so far from the tower operator there was a "whistle punk" that used an electronic device that let the "donkey puncher" or tower operator know what he wanted him to do to get the load hooked up. The signals went as follows: one for stop, two for back, three for forward and four for slack. These whistles would echo over the whole mountainside, and if the "punk" got too carried away with his whistling there would be a confrontation with the "donkey puncher" in the crummie ride home that evening, because his ears would be shot at the end of a twelve hour shift.

We were picked up at three-thirty am sharp; we crawled into the crummie and headed due east to the setting. The boss apologized for the setting being so far from home base and almost didn't bid on it because of this fact. The men were packed in with each row seating three men and three seats not including the driver and shotgun seat. There were eight of us, and I could sense the old timers were irritated at the long drive to work. We were heading

CHAPTER 5

for the Three Sisters Mountain range, and the trip would take a couple of hours to get there, arriving just at day break.

There were several men in the crew I could tell right off were going to be interesting to observe. Emile was old for this type of work, at around forty to forty-five years old, and like a lot of loggers, he used snuff instead of cigarettes which were banned in this type of work. He carried his Copenhagen can in his top pocket which had worn a permanent circle in the material of his shirt. He was our foreman. Old Dan was by far the senior man amongst us and was at least sixty years old, but looked seventy or more. He had been a logger most of his life and lost an eye and the use of an arm in the process; with a twisted back he worked the landing and did a great job for a man in his condition. He never complained and he had the most steadfast disposition of any one there. He had a large family and so was locked into this dead end job at his age. I knew the boss kept him on not only for his calm attitude but his loyal service over the years.

The crummie pulled over to the side of the dirt road and one of the men jumped out, grabbed two canvas water bags and trotted to a natural spring falling off the cliff to our left. He filled the bags, returned to the van and jumped in. "Best tasting water on the mountain," he said, and it would prove true before the morning was done. We finally arrived and we emptied the crummie as if the dang thing was on fire. The boss wanted us to get cracking right off and didn't want us to waste any time farting around. We were directed to the top of the setting right below the tower where we were given some advice about staying alive. First, don't ever stand under the mainline or haul back, second, don't ever stand in the bite; third, don't get between the load and the tower; and fourth, keep an eye out for widow makers or loose limbs ready to fall from any skag trees left behind. The rest we would pick up along the way. I didn't realize it at the time, but choker setting is the most dangerous job in the world, excelling deep sea fishing and crabbing off Alaska, which most people think is the worst job alive. Here I was with my new tin hat, new clothes, suspenders, and gloves, ready to go.

The huge diesel engine that ran the tower fired up and we were about to embark on a journey I would never forget. I surveyed the mountainside below us; there were logs strewn every-which-a-way over the whole mountain. Some of the logs were small but most were over six to ten feet in diameter; one-log-loads, the truck drivers called them. Enough wood in one load to build a complete house. Emile punked out four whistles and the massive cable in front of us slacked down and we grabbed the chokers, one for Rick, and one for me. Rick showed me how to slide the bell up the choker and take the nubbin end and shove, or sometimes dig it under the log, jump over the log and retrieve the nubbin, jump back with it and insert it into the bell, run for cover and yell "All clear." Beep, beep, beep and the logs were hiked up to the landing for Dan to release them and send them back for another load. Beep and the rigging stopped. Beep, beep, beep, beep and the rigging slacked down and the process started all over again.

The beginning of the rows was the worst because we didn't get a chance to rest between loads before they were back for more run, jump, climb, push, etc. To add to the miseries we endured, we had to contend with the friggin' Manzanita bushes entangled throughout the whole setting. Tripping over these two to three-foot high bushes always brought out the colorful language I soon picked up on the mountain.

CHAPTER 5

The brute force of the tower always amazed me and I saw many chokers snapped like a string when a log got jammed in between some stumps. After a few hundred uses, these chokers would look more like huge corkscrews dangling from the main line rather than nice straight new ones we preferred. Trying to push a corkscrew under a log was a challenge not appreciated in any way. These ones usually had the sharp steel strands sticking out of them that punctured the fingers in a most painful way, cloth gloves or not. We had reached the bottom of the first row about two hundred yards from the tower, and were enjoying the short rest, as Emile disconnected the tail holt, and with our help, lugged the three pieces it broke down to over another fifty feet or so to set up the next row. They had retrieved the mainline onto the yarder and substituted it with a straw line for easy maneuvering while we set up the new row. This straw line was only a half inch in diameter and was used to pull the main line back in after the tail holt was set up and ready. It was a lot easier to move through the Manzanitas and over logs than the two-inch diameter monster. Emil spotted a sturdy looking stump and began notching the back side with an axe to keep the cable sling anchoring the tailholt from slipping over the stump and wiping out everything in the bite.

After completing the flip-over, as this operation was called, we broke for lunch and none too soon for me. I was shot, entirely wiped out, emptied, and ready to quit. Emile called for the water bag and they tied it to the choker rigging and lowered it to us via high lead express. It really was the sweetest tasting water I have ever had, and even now with all the bottled water choices available, none comes close. I wolfed down my lunch and wished for more, drank some coffee out of my stainless thermos and stretched out on a smooth log for a rest. It seemed like seconds as the whistle blew again, and up the mountain we hiked through the Manzanitas again to the top of the new row where it began all over again. We had made three rows before it got too dark to see properly.

I fell asleep in the crummie on the way down the mountain to which I got my share of ribbing from the old timers. I crawled into the shower when we got home and ate a bit and fell into bed. I couldn't sleep because my legs just vibrated and I couldn't stop them. Two seconds later the alarm went off and we were at it again. The vibrating stopped after three days of misery until I finally fell into a coma-like sleep and rested. I was cramming sandwiches into my lunch pail as well as stuffing them in the lid and an extra one in my pocket. The coffee thermos was slung over my shoulder with a leather thong. It was an art form, pouring coffee into a cup in the crummie as we traversed the bumpy dirt roads and not spilling a drop. You had to get into the sway of it and as your body rocked in a rhythm you could pull it off quite nicely.

Standing halfway down a row one day, we were confronted with the most screwed up kinky choker we ever saw. It only got worse as we went along. Finally, Emile said, "I'll fix that kinky son-of-a-bitch. Wayne, pull the damn thing over there by that huge stump and wrap the miserable thing on it for me." I did as I was told, and waited as he whistled for the donkey puncher to haul it out. The diesel wound up and the slack eased out till the choker was as tight as an "E" string on a guitar. You could tell the puncher was wondering' "What the heck?" Emile hit the whistle once more and that's all it took for the puncher to slam it into a lower gear and let her rip. Wham, Emile grinned and said, "That's the last we'll see of that mother." He pulled his Copenhagen out and emptied the

CHAPTER 5

last of it into a wad and stuffed it in his bottom lip, took the lid and frisbeed it down the mountainside with the delight of a small child.

I lost twenty pounds the first week and knew why we wore suspenders; it's because my pants and waist kept changing so often my britches would fall off if I had a belt on. I finally got the hang of it and I didn't quit after all, gaining the respect of the men. Apparently they were used to city slickers coming up for the big money but few cutting the mustard. Rick had done this before so knew what he was getting into. It didn't get easier, just more tolerable.

We logged through all kinds of weather: snow, sleet, hail, blazing hot and freezing cold, and nothing stopped us. If it snowed, we lit fires up and down the rows and ran over between loads to thaw out and eye the next log we would tie off for the next run. On one occasion when we were logging an exceptionally steep grade, I took a few moments to relax. The ground, as usual, was covered with the ever tangling Manzanitas, so I jumped onto a flat stump to get free of them. There was a large outcropping of rocks halfway up the slide and as the load reached them, some broke loose and came rolling down on us. They were the size of large beach balls and some larger than that. I, on the other hand, didn't know because I was looking in the wrong direction. I was looking at my boss down the slope standing outside his pickup surveying the next cut. He was parked on a dirt road about a hundred yards below us. He began waving frantically at me and I thought, "How friendly." I waved back and then felt the breeze of a washing machine sized boulder whizzing past my ear not two inches from my head. I instinctively squatted down and spun around to see several smaller ones on the way. I jumped behind the stump I had been standing on which made a good hiding place until the danger passed. Rick's face was ashen white and he started ranting at me for almost getting killed and how would he tell my parents etc., etc. I said it wasn't my idea and calm down before we come to blows over it. My boss was laying on the hood of his truck either from relief or passed out from shock. This was my first close call.

Saturday came, our first day off, and Rick and I were laying back in our apartment relaxing when we noticed two girls carrying stuff past our window and up to the place above ours. They had rented the upstairs flat and were moving in. I told Rick things were looking up. I asked the girls if they needed help with the larger stuff, but they declined since they were just finishing, but said thanks anyway. They were two college students working on their degrees and teaching at the local grade school in Roseburg. One was a gorgeous knock-out blond, tall and built like an athlete. The other was a brunette, a little stockier but with a fantastic personality. The blond said she was engaged to a marine and the brunette single and proud of it. I tried to get Rick to ask one of them out so we could double date them once we got to know them better. He was naturally shy and just suggesting it put him in a dither. He turned red and got angry from just asking him. When he was around girls, he usually clammed up and just sat there like a bump on a log making everyone uncomfortable from his lack of mixing in.

 We were invited upstairs to the girls' apartment for dinner the following Saturday evening and I was looking forward to the date. They knew I played the guitar and asked me to bring it along when we came. I said, "Sure." The evening came and Rick and I hoofed it

CHAPTER 5

upstairs, guitar and wine in hand. The girls had cooked a fantastic roast beef dinner with all the trimmings and with the chilled wine, we all settled down to a scrumptious meal. Despite Rick's one-word answers to the girls' queries, we had a great time. The blond was Tina and the brunette was Brenda. Both were roommates in college and both had no idea we were just in high school, a fact we managed to, astutely, conceal from them. I never saw the marine that Tina was supposed to be engaged to and I wondered if he was just a ruse to keep guys at bay since she was a striking woman and was hit on all the time from guys everywhere. We became good friends and we took in a movie once in a while on Saturday evenings but never seemed to have enough time to really get involved in a more serious way. I would have loved to have a closer relationship with Tina but held off when I felt I was getting too close, just in case she actually was engaged. I thought she would tell me if she wanted things to get a little deeper. I never knew if the big bad marine would show up and put me in my place.

The summer quickly passed, and the time in Roseburg all too soon came to a halt. I was now 220 lbs. and hard as nails. I remember walking down the main drag with Tina and Brenda and feeling my oats. I ran up to a parking meter and putting my palms on the top, kicked up into a hand stand on top of the meter and then did a couple of push-ups before dismounting. Just the thought of it now kills me.

We packed our gear and wished the girls well. After a hug or two we were heading home via San Francisco, where I wanted to buy a new tailor-made suit. My aunt Hazel lived there and she owned a hair salon at the end of Powell Street where the tram cars turn around. She put us up for a couple of days and, of course, had to introduce us to the Barbary Coast. Steaks were on the menu and she would only let us order rare ones. She said any steak cooked past rare was ruined. I didn't like my meat that way but since she was paying, I conceded. Aunt Hazel was in every way like "Mame" In the old movie with Roslyn Russell. She was pretty, lived alone and liked a good time. The restaurant we were eating at was situated right in the middle of the Barbary Coast district and since pirate times was known for its wild and notorious exploits. It wasn't any surprise when the waitress who tended our table was well endowed and topless. Hazel just smiled and ordered her rare steak from the menu. I noticed her amusement as Rick and I squirmed in our seats. I tried to keep my eyes on the menu and not on the bouncing boobs two inches from my nose. A cold sweat broke out on my forehead and I swore the temperature raised several degrees in there over the next five minutes. I managed to stammer out my order and passed the problem off to Rick. Mr. Shy-guy turned a crimson red and added a new dimension to the term red light district, of which I felt we were now in. I think his glow brightened up the interior by fifty lumens. We managed to get our orders in and settled back for our meal. Watching the topless waitresses roaming the floor opened up a line of dialog consisting of comparisons, such as watermelons, zucchinis, honeydews, and grapefruits. I think there was a set of fried eggs in there somewhere. All in all, the dinner was great and the experience priceless.

    I got measured for my suit the following day, and after I paid the man we set off for home once again. It was six weeks before my suit arrived and in that time I had gained enough weight that the suit didn't fit. I had picked one out I had seen James Bond wearing in the movie "Goldfinger." It was a three-piece grey plaid

CHAPTER 5

beauty that I never got to wear. I had a pocket full of money and a head full of memories. Life was good and I was ready for my last year of school.

Unbeknown to me, Tina had written me a long letter and mailed it to my parent's house, the only home address I had. In it she stated how much she really missed me, and that she wanted to tell me how much she loved me but could never get up the courage to do so. She wished I hadn't left, and she said she had broken up with her fiancé "the marine" and that she missed me so very much. Life has a wicked way of throwing you a curve ball once in a while and this one totally blew me away.

CHAPTER 6

It was my junior year at school and I had settled into a regime that I felt rewarding and also enjoyable too. My work in the school garage brought various challenges to light. My supervisor was a short man we called "Pops." He couldn't be more than five ft. in height and he drove around in a reconditioned '56 Ford pick-up. He had put cushions on his seat to give him enough height to see out the windshield. It was comical watching him get in and out of his truck since it dwarfed him in size and a VW would have been more suitable for his stature.

He was a frugal manager and did things I really didn't approve of. If there was one thing that irritated me the most, it was having to use old gaskets over again. The cost of new gaskets was minimal in comparison to doing the job over again because the seal leaked.

We had several flunkies helping in the garage doing odd jobs such as cleaning parts and sweeping up. There was one who thought he knew it all and didn't hesitate to tell us at every turn. I was doing an overhaul and needed the oil pump and screen cleaned prior to re-installing it. The " Whizz Kid" knew how to do this and without asking first, started a chain of events soon to escalate into a major problem. He filled a drain pan, one we use for removing sump oil into, with gasoline, then placed the oil pump assembly into it and scrubbed all the crud off the outside surface. He knew the screen had to be also cleared so came up with the brilliant idea of burning it off first. He picked the pump up and walked outside so as not to catch the shop on fire. He placed the pump on the ground and set it on fire. He hadn't counted on the trail of gas he left behind himself as he transferred the pump outdoors. The fire quickly spread back into the shop as if a fuse had been laid down to set it on fire on purpose. Flames shot skyward when they finally reached the drain pan and by then Mr. Whizz Kid was running around frantically screaming and waving his arms in the air for help. The flames engulfed the wall of the shop and were spreading at a healthy rate and if it hadn't been for the dairy guys passing the shop at that moment I am sure the whole thing would have burnt to the ground. They grabbed some extinguishers and had the flames under control within a few minutes.

Pops was in town getting parts when this all transpired and I was in class. It just went to show the futility of using old parts over again when we should have installed a new pump and screen. The price of an overhaul included all these items, but it was a method Pops used to kept his costs within budget and increase his profits.

Most of the shops had a jeep to use for running parts or hauling equipment around. The jeeps were WWII surplus ones and they had a few trailers, which used to be munitions carriers, too. Our jeep was the best, mainly because I kept it that way. Groundskeeping had a jeep and so did the dairy and farm shop.

The weekends were boring most of the time so a few of us kids decided to take the jeeps over the back road into the valley behind us. The dirt road was there for the maintenance to drive back in the hills to check the tanks and pipes that fed the schools water supply. Once you breached the top of the hill, you had all those acres where you could do whatever your heart desired. Mine and Jim's hearts wanted to trip as far back into the hills as we could go. Walking wasn't in the plan so we decided to stash the jeep behind the boys'

CHAPTER 6

dorm until after church when we would sneak up the back road and beyond.

I had filled the jeep with gas so had plenty to make the trip. Once we topped the hill, we put it into four wheel drive and cruised on down the road. We came across some dicey situations but managed to get through. This is what made it fun, the challenge of getting there. In the distance, we spotted some buildings and decided to investigate. By driving through some dry river beds and sandy knolls, we finally came upon an old movie set. There were log houses and store fronts and other buildings to create a frontier setting. Of course, there were only the fronts of these buildings, no rears and only a few sides. It was our private "Movie Valley" and that's what we dubbed it from then on. On the way back we made a mental note of where it was and how we could get back to it when we wanted.

It was still early so we decided to try to climb the mountain between us and the school. Jim was driving so he headed towards the slope he felt we had the best chance of attaining the top from. We were heading straight up at a 45-degree angle and soon the engine couldn't take the strain and bogged down to a stop. Jim got the gears into low four and we gave it another shot. We gained another 20 yards or so when the four wheels started spinning. We were engulfed in scrub oak and bushes with an occasional yucca plant to maneuver around also. By now we were pointing straight up and in danger of rolling over. I told Jim we couldn't go any further up so had to turn around in this crap and work our way back down to the valley below. The trouble was if we turned the wheels and moved back we would roll for sure before we straightened up and drove down. I happened to be on the uphill side of the jeep so had the brainstorm of standing on the foot hold on the outside of the cab and holding on to the windshield, then stretch myself out like an outrigger canoe thus changing the center of gravity and enabling us to get down. There was definitely a sphincter factor involved in this hair-brained maneuver and I would register it around a 9 out of10. Jim started his little laugh again which he did on occasion when things got scary. I wanted to tell him not to but didn't want the situation to get any worse that it already was so held on and said "hit it". So with me hanging off the side of the jeep at an almost level angle to the ground, Jim popped the clutch and swung the jeep around as if it was the best-laid plan. We made it down safely and drove back to the school with no further problems. Whenever I drove down the dirt road with a friend or passenger, I point out the place Jim and I drove the jeep. I always got the same reaction: "No way in hell". I felt the same too as I look up the slope and wonder how the blazes did we get up there.

Bud Feldkamp was a year ahead of me and hung out with the same crowd as Jim and I. We were discussing the back road and the fun tearing down it in the jeeps. He fancied himself a racer type and wanted to join in the fun so we managed to acquire a couple of vehicles and headed up the back road. Once over the top we had a winding road ahead of us for about half mile before it ran out and petered out into a trail with no visible direction either way. There were only a few curves broad enough to pass so you had to plan your moves pretty well to win a race down the back road. We punched it and were off. We flew down the road blowing a billow of dust behind us as we slid around the curves. I passed him on the second turn and he never caught me for the rest of the race. Bud wasn't

CHAPTER 6

a happy camper and wanted a rematch so we did it again. I beat him again and this just infuriated him worse. I felt two races were enough so called it quits for the day. This scenario continued for many weeks and each time he came up second. Graduation was fast approaching and he would be gone forever and this wouldn't do.

He challenged me one more time so the race was set and we once more lined up and ready to go. For the last time, we punched off and hurled ourselves down the dirt motor cross. I could sense he was pushing himself beyond his capabilities and was extra careful not to let him cause me to lose control. In one second, we were neck in neck and the next he was gone. I looked back just in time to see his Jeep careening off the road and down the side of the hill. Bud was thrown free and landed on his back. The Jeep continued to roll a few more times until it stopped right side up at the bottom of the slope. He was holding his leg and grimacing pretty intensely. I helped him into my Jeep and raced to the nurses' station in the administration building. I said, " Bud, you had better come up with a good story as to how you broke your leg or you and I will be expelled for what we did." He agreed and devised some outlandish tale. It must have worked because I never heard another thing about it until graduation.

Bud was the only senior that graduated with a cast on and whenever I see his picture in the school annual, I get a chuckle over it. The weird thing about this story is the fact that Bud went on to be a successful dentist at Loma Linda University School of Dentistry. He opened up several offices and became well known as a superb businessman. His passion is racing and his wealth affords him the luxury of building race cars and racing them at various tracks around the country. No matter how good he gets though, he will never be able to turn back the clock and beat the garage jeep racing hell-bent for leather down the dirt road back of the Academy in Newbury Park.

Hunger is a sickness most of the guys in the dorm suffered from most of the time. There was an A&W stand a few miles down the highway that used to sneak burgers and fries plus gallons of root beer to us behind the boys' dormitory. We would place an order and if it were large enough, they would deliver it for free. It wasn't uncommon for a student to run from room to room taking orders until he reached the minimum amount for an order. On this occasion, there was no A&W to order from because they had torn it down to build an overpass across the highway. There was a definite period of mourning after the demise of our beloved A&W. This didn't alleviate the problem at hand and hungry bellies must be filled.

The conversation turned to the cafeteria and the goodies stashed away there that we could have for the taking if only there were a few guys brave enough to get in there to retrieve them.

We decided to draw straws to see who these brave few would be. Unfortunately, I fell into the category of the lucky few. Now there was only one night watchman on duty and he was pretty old and he spent a lot of time parked across the highway by the farm shop where he caught a few winks in the front seat of his cruiser. We had watched enough spy movies to realize we needed to wear black clothes and probably blacken our faces to lessen the chances of being spotted.

Sneaking out of the dorm was no problem since a lot of the guys had jobs requiring late or extra early departure times. The dairy had milking and the farm shop had plowing etc. No, the trick

CHAPTER 6

was to keep a watch on the girls' dorm. They were guarded like they were watching Fort Knox. There were alarms on the windows and doors and any other orifice that might be compromised. Fortunately, the cafeteria wasn't as guarded as the girls' dorm. We could pick the locks on the outer doors and hopefully the storage room inside. The caper was a cinch and we were quickly heading for the cafeteria. The outer doors were smooth and soon we found ourselves inside and at the storage room door. The sweat began dripping down my brow from the ski mask I had borrowed for the occasion. Mike was puffing too as he tried to pick the lock into the food area. We weren't having much luck and as we were stymied there, the door rattled and in came the night watchman. We hit the floor. He hadn't seen us and began his perfunctory duties of checking doors and shining his flashlight around the perimeter for anything out of place. My heart almost stopped as we lay there as quiet as dead people. Suddenly the watchman, who thought he was all alone, broke wind. This wasn't just a little squeaker but a full on rattle-your-britches King Kong of farts. I swear he must have dropped three inches of his waistline with that one. Of course, the guys couldn't contain themselves and all burst out laughing like idiots. There was nothing we could do to contain ourselves and the cat was out.

The night watchman dropped his flashlight from shock, and we all headed for an exit, cracking up as we ran for our lives. I wasn't about to leave empty handed so grabbed a sack of apples by the store room door. Running with a fifty-pound bag isn't easy but determination won out. Returning to the room we all assembled and exchanged stories. I cut the sack open but found it full of onions. A miserable disappointment to what I had hoped for.

There would be an investigation and we had to keep our mouths shut or we all would be expelled. I had to take the evidence out and get rid of it. Early the following morning I took the sack of onions in the Jeep and dumped them down the side of the dirt road just over the rise from the school. We never were found out and the story of the big onion caper was a staple story for many years after. I met a woman many years later that lived in Thousand Oaks and she used to ride horseback through those very hills behind the academy. I related the great onion caper to her and she burst out laughing when I told her how I had thrown the evidence over the side of the dirt road. She said, to this day, there is still a wild onion patch thriving where I had tossed them forty years ago.

CHAPTER 7

Mom was in her bedroom crying as my dad and I walked into the house. We had just returned from purchasing my first new/used car. It was an Olds Cutlass 1964 model with four on the floor and bucket seats center console and painted a dark maroon. They hadn't come up with the 442 model yet, that was to come the following year. I asked Mom why the tears and she said she didn't want to see me entering the world of monthly payments this early in life. I didn't understand then why the fuss but I do now. Mom was wise concerning money because she had to make do raising five kids and supporting her mother also all on Dad's salary. She had been doing this ever since I can remember. Dad, on the other hand, had a more cavalier attitude and usually said, "We'll manage somehow". The somehow was Mom's frugality that kept us afloat. She wiped her tears and came outside to admire my new purchase. Mom let us know how she felt but wasn't prone to laying guilt trips on us after the fact. Her opinion was voiced; "Now let's enjoy our new purchase." She liked my vinyl seats and hated with a passion the velour seat covers. She referred to them, later in life, as Velcro seats; ones you had to un-stick yourself from to get in or out.

I had built my first car from scratch. Walking home from grade school I used to take a short-cut through a fig orchard. At the rear of the orchard was a 31 Ford five-window coupe body sitting in the weeds. The fenders were lying beside it and the radiator shell was propped inside. The orchard had been abandoned for years and weeds had engulfed the entire lot. I checked with the neighbors and no one knew if the owners were ever present. There wasn't a house, only the property. After a lengthy search I finally figured it was up for grabs. I opened the side door and stepped inside. The roof had rotted off where the material top piece used to be. There were the ribs of wood still there but nothing else. I was standing in the weeds since there was no frame, only the body. I pushed up on the roof structure and with a lot of effort broke the body free from the weeds. It was dangling around me like a bell and I was the clapper. I walked home that way, about half a mile. I'm sure the neighbors had a laugh at this thing walking down the middle of the street with weeds hanging off the perimeter and two legs walking along like Fred Flintstone except with tennis shoes on.

I reached home and deposited it in our front yard while I retreated back to the field and picked up the rest of the parts. I managed to find a frame and started to put the pieces together. My dad was an electrician by trade but was proficient in all phases of metal work. He welded and that was the key for me right then. He worked at a fabricating plant in Hollywood and as I made cardboard brackets to fit body to frame, etc, I would give these mock-ups to him each morning and he would fabricate them for me into metal at work in his spare time.

I was in eighth grade at the time and was fascinated with mechanics ever since my dad, my brother Rob, and my brother-in-law Frank switched out a straight eight Pontiac engine in my sister's '48 sedan. I wanted a Hemi engine and picked one up at the wrecking yard on Main St. in Los Angeles for $100.00, a Chrysler " Fire Dome" 330 cubic inch beauty. I managed to acquire a Ford three-speed transmission and a "banjo" rear end. These weren't the best choices, but I had limited funds and this is what I could afford.

CHAPTER 7

I didn't know what to do about the funky top so decided to cut it off. I welded the doors closed and turned a 5 window coupe into a full-on roadster. I had a hacksaw blade to do the job with and with the help of my other brother-in-law Ted, I inserted a couple of large nails through the hacksaw blades end holes and we walked around the roof as we sawed back and forth. The panel under the deck lid was missing so Dad fabricated me another that fit in perfectly. I hit the wrecking yard again and got the tail light assemblies from a Pontiac Tempest. They were flat and worked fine. I would work on this project night and day and when really strapped for cash would put the bite on Mom for a $20.00 here or $50.00 there. She always came through and it wasn't until years later she told me it was no small sacrifice to keep me off the streets and out of trouble.

I found myself fast asleep under the car while lying on a creeper many times, waking up at way past midnight, cold and hungry. My grandfather who was in his late eighties at the time helped me cut down a Ford coupe seat to fit the width of my roadster. I had it painted canary yellow and it looked sharp. I had to use motorcycle front fenders since someone had managed to sneak into our back yard and steal one of my full fenders. All in all, it looked pretty nice especially since it was done by a 14-year-old kid who really didn't give a damn what people thought of it. He loved it and couldn't wait to try her out.

I needed a gas tank so found two five-gallon drums and cut the tops out. I set them top to top and welded the two top lips together to make a ten-gallon tank. It worked fine except for a small leak in the weld. I emptied the tank of gas and knew better than weld it with all the explosive fumes inside so filled it with water figuring the fumes were all displaced by the water. As soon as I touched the flame to weld, POW, the tank blew up in my face, spewing water all over me and buckling the tank beyond being usable again. Fortunately, there weren't a lot of fumes left to blow up and no injuries incurred but I was lucky that day.

I finally got most of the pieces together enough to fire it up and take it for a run. I cranked her over and she came to life. I revved it up a couple of times and she sounded sweet. I had to make a few minor adjustments to the carburetor but no problem; she purred and the feeling of complete satisfaction I felt at that moment cannot be put into words. I eased her into first gear and slowly let out the clutch. She shot backward instead of forwards and it creeped me out for a second. What the hell was this now? I put it in reverse and it went forwards. Hell, I had three speeds back and one heck of a first gear forwards. The old Ford banjo rear ends could be accidently installed upside down and this is what I had done. It didn't take long and I had it flipped over and away I went. I have only had that feeling I experienced then a precious few times in my life, and the words I conjure up now can't do justice to the reality. My cousins and I used to cruise the beaches from Palos Verdes to El Porto in this yellow canary and the fun we used to have out did any trip you could take on any of the drugs prevalent on the streets at that time.

It wasn't long before I had to beef up the Cutlass' engine. It had plenty of spunk, but it was never enough to do what I felt it should do. I pulled the stock engine out and dropped in a 421 cubic inch Pontiac with roller cam and dual quads. There was no comparison. The Pontiac would light the tires up until you burnt them off the rims. Top speed was not readable since my speedometer only went

CHAPTER 7

to 120 MPH. I twisted the needle way past that mark and could only guess at what speed I was running.

I was attending a college in La Sierra, a few miles southwest of Riverside, California. A friend of mine, Scott, was visiting and needed to get back to his high school in Lynnwood to pick up his car. We had to go down the Santa Ana Canyon way because the freeway wasn't built yet. I told him I would be happy to take him if he could take the ride. We pulled out of the school parking lot and I nailed it. The instant acceleration snapped your head back and you could feel your body burying itself into the bucket seats as the car shot down the highway. Each gear restarted the feeling over again and when you reached fourth, you were lost in the whole experience to complete madness. It was real late at night so little traffic was on the road. We never used our seat belts in those days but due to the radical maneuvers I managed, we felt impelled to put them on.

As any kid will tell you, speed is a narcotic as pervasive as any drug on the market. Your heart starts pumping harder and your cheeks get flushed and burning. You begin to breathe in short gasps, uncontrollably, and your palms sweat a little just to let you know you're on the edge. I drifted around curves and almost went airborne over rises. I kept looking in the rearview mirror to see if a cop had picked me up on radar and was following me. None yet, thank goodness. Scott fell in love with my Cutlass at that time and little did we know he would buy it from me a year or two later. He would live some stories of his own behind the wheel of a full-on speed machine.

We pulled into his high school parking lot after twenty minutes of white knuckling, breathtaking, life-threatening craziness. I would like to be remembered as a level-headed kid who did the right thing all the time but as I reminisce I fall short of that ideal by a mile. I cringe at the things I survived and I know it was only due to my mother's prayers and God's forbearance.

I think the reason I beefed up the Cutlass was that, prior to the incident at La Sierra, I had attended a reunion at Newbury Academy and met my old nemesis, Bud, there. The cast was gone, but the feelings of resentment were only burned deeper into his soul and he had to rectify the situation or else die trying. He was driving his new Chevy Chevelle with a four-speed and Quad, dual exhaust, and all the goodies. He had to race me again, his Chevelle against my Cutlass. I knew my Cutlass was overweight as his Chevy was a lot lighter than the Olds, but to rid Bud of his demons I agreed. We raced a quarter mile just outside the school grounds and Bud took me by a fender not only once but several times. He was ecstatic and I was happy he finally could get over his manic obsession that was eating him up. I never saw Bud after that and even though we were neighbors living in Redlands, California years later, and our kids went to the same school together, he never relinquished his disdain for losing the" Le Mans" down the dirt road, behind the Academy, so many years ago.

Soon after I left college, I applied for a job at Ray Vane Chrysler located on Pacific Coast Highway in Torrance, California. They hired me on as their used car mechanic. You can imagine the fun I had in 1969 and 1970 tuning up the trade-ins and test driving them prior to putting them on the lot for resale. We had Barracudas and Challengers, GTX's and Chargers, all the muscle cars you could dream for. I remember one time an older man driving his

CHAPTER 7

GTX into the lot and trading it in for a less aggressive car. He had a 426 Hemi engine with dual quads and the rock crusher four-speed transmission with the pistol grip shifter and Dana posi rear end. Hell, if I'd known he wanted a less aggressive car I would have traded him for my VW and we would've both been happy. I remember taking the car out for a test run and actually having trouble keeping the tires from breaking loose. The car was every kid's dream, but it was the old codgers that could afford them and then complain about their aggressiveness. Life isn't fair.

I had another car I was working on, a '70 Challenger, bright orange and suffering an engine misfire. I had diagnosed the problem as a faulty carburetor and had to do an overhaul on it to clean it up and get it functioning again. Once I had the carburetor replaced I took the car out for a spin. I put it into first gear and eased out onto Pacific Coast Highway. The engine was still coughing and sputtering a bit so figured I had better floor it to blow out all the excess gas that had accumulated in the engine from before. The engine sprang to life and I was flying down the road before I knew it. Coming from the opposite side of the road, on the other side of the divided highway island, was a cop car. He immediately put on his lights and pointed to the side of the road. I figured I was screwed so drove on down to a turnabout and started heading the same way as the officer. Before I got two blocks down the road, the police car was coming back the same way I had been going full speed with his siren on and he was pissed. He saw me on the other side of the street and flipped me off and sped up more to try and catch up to me. I knew I was in for it now and I could tell he thought I was attempting to evade him and escape. Two thoughts ran through my mind at that moment. One, I could stop and wait for him and probably get arrested for evading arrest, or two, run like hell and try to get away. I opted for the latter and punched it to the floor. The Challenger rose to the occasion and roared south spewing black smoke out the exhaust for a second or two and then settled down to a throbbing growl. I had successfully cleared out the carburetor, now what? My little pea brain told me to turn into the residential area right next to the highway and hide somewhere. I hung a right and zoomed to the top of the hill, covered with homes, and found an old deserted church and slipped into the weed encrusted parking lot and turned off the engine. I got out and said to myself that I had better time myself and don't go anywhere for at least a half an hour. I checked my watch and waited. The half hour seemed like two days. I never would have waited that long if I hadn't checked my watch. After an eternity finally passed by I got back in the Challenger and slowly worked my way back down the hill.

Trying to hide in a bright orange car is no easy task. I hit the main road and decided to enter the lot through the back entrance. I pulled up alongside the buildings that constituted the repair facility which was like a big "L" shape, with all the bays facing the square parking structure. The doors of the shops were all open and in front of each one was a mechanic standing there looking out into the parking lot. I eased on around to the transmission shop and rolled down the window to speak to the mechanic standing there. I said, "What's going on?"

He said, "Wayne, a cop, just this second, went tearing out the main entrance yelling about an orange car he was chasing. He said he was going to nail the guy driving it and he knew it came from here." Apparently the cop was burning donuts with his cruiser in

CHAPTER 7

the parking lot and the rubber he left behind attested to his total lack of restraint in this whole affair. I would have been dead meat if I had returned ten seconds sooner. I quietly went to the very back of the lot, parked the Challenger and didn't touch it for a week.

CHAPTER 8

Chief was a Choctaw Indian and worked at the local auto parts store. He was big in stature and always had a faraway look in his eye. As far as I know he wasn't a chief but he liked to be called that and so I did. We hit it off right away and swapped a lot of stories about our youth. We were both barely twenty, and as he put it, in our "crazy years". I never knew when he was pulling my leg, but it didn't matter because the stories were interesting and colorful.

He drove a Ford pickup 1955 vintage with a 392 Chrysler Hemi engine. It was ragged on the outside, but it had a heart of pure muscle. He was raised in Wichita, Kansas and still had kin there that he wanted me to meet some day. We had ideas about going back together and looking for classic cars on the "res", as he put it. The reservation covered many miles and there were old cars abandoned all over the place where with the right equipment, we could pull them out, bring them back to California and sell them for a sweet profit. He said if you weren't Indian or with the one you had better not get caught back in the hills of the "res" or you might never come out. He wasn't kidding. Even though we dallied with the thought of doing this, we never got around to actually doing it.

Chief had an uncle not too much older than himself who was driving to Kansas and asked me if I wanted to go. I said I would and after I packed a few items and my guitar we headed out. He drove a white Chevy pick-up and always had a whiskey bottle stashed under the driver's side of the seat. He called it his

"Libation of life" and by the way he sucked it down, he would live forever. I have heard about Indians not being able to hold their liquor so it amazed me to see this one constantly guzzling the stuff and still drive in a straight line. We would stop every once in a while so he could refresh the libation, which amounted to about every third gas stop.

We arrived at the front door of A.C. Wilson's place in Wichita, at around two in the morning. It didn't occur to uncle to let the inhabitants sleep; he just pounded on the front door till A.C. opened it and the hullabaloo began. The hugs and profanities were many and sincere. The fridge was opened and the beer flowed. By the time the sons-of-a-bitches and low-down-rotten-cowpokes, you jive-ass's, and a few other terms of endearment, a lot more descriptive, were exchanged, I was a bonafide part of the family.

The guitar was produced and the singing began. Now A.C. had three kids and no wife; she split with some other fella a few years ago and A.C. raised his children alone. There was Kathy the eldest, around thirteen at the time, then came Rita, who was about seven, and then Buck, who was still in three-cornered pants. A.C. and Kathy smoked like chimneys and since she pulled more than her weight, I guess A.C. just looked the other way when she decided to light up.

Kathy was the surrogate mother who did the shopping and changed Buck whenever he need it, or whenever we told her to "cause it was getting a little ripe in here". There was a lot of love in this "maladjusted" family and even though he had to do it on his own, he did the best he could, under the circumstances. A.C. wasn't like Uncle. He drank like a fish, mostly beer, and couldn't walk a straight line if his life depended on it, anytime. The kids loved the

CHAPTER 8

singing and guitar playing and we kept the neighbors up till the wee hours of the morning.

We finally ran out of liquor and consciousness about sun-up and sacked out anywhere we found a dry spot and soft cushions. I woke up around noon and staggered to the kitchen where A.C. was making coffee and breakfast. He was a short man, slender built and endowed with rich Indian features. He always had a pleasant disposition and said "Howdy Partner" in a most honest rendition of the term and I knew it was sincere. I said, "Hey, A.C. where's Uncle?"

"Oh, he lit out about an hour ago," he said.

"When is he coming back?" I queried.

"Don't think he is," A.C. said. "He left your stuff in the living room and took off." I knew Indians had some peculiar ways and I had just fallen into a giant one right then. I never saw Uncle again and wondered to this day what caused him to run off. A.C. said, "Don't worry, things will work out fine, just you wait and see."

He had to get to work at the Cudahy meatpacking plant but would be home around five. He would snag some steaks under his shirt for dinner and we would have a BBQ when he got home. Snagging steaks was a way of life for old A.C. and he did other things too, to keep his kids and I fed. I could tell he liked me and wanted me around for the company and to keep the kids entertained; I had 87 cents in my pocket and wasn't going anywhere for some time. A.C. drove an old beat-up Dodge pickup painted blue and sporting pom-poms around the perimeter of the cab ceiling. It was old enough that the hood opened from the sides instead of the front like most do now, and he loved it.

He had some time off and asked me if I wanted to travel a bit and meet some of his people. I said I would like to and after we packed up the kids and the guitar and the diapers and grub and, of course, the beer, we set our sights on the Kiamichi Mountains in Oklahoma. Now with A.C. smoking and Kathy smoking, I thought why not do something I had wanted to do for some time and give it a try too. I fancied myself more a roll-your-own kind of guy so at the next gas stop, got a can of Prince Albert tobacco and a pack of Zigzag papers to see if I had the makings of a real cowboy. I had rolled a joint or two in high school so figured no big deal. A.C. said maybe I shouldn't twist the ends shut 'cause it might look suspicious if a cop pulled us over. I thought that solid advice since we were down two six packs by then and working on the next.

We arrived at a distant relatives' log house outside Poteau, Oklahoma. As we drove up the dirt road to his front porch, I caught a glimpse of an old man sitting in a rocking chair enjoying the morning sunrise. A.C. said his name was Davy Crockett Warren and he was the great, great grandson of Davy himself. He was over 100 years old and still getting around on his own power. I was introduced and welcomed country style, which is with sincere warmth and affection. He was a colorful man with long hair down past his shoulders and even though his hair was thin, he wore it with pride and distinction.

There was a Folgers Coffee can beside his rocking chair into which he expurgated a chew of tobacco. He had a plug in his pocket for which he often reached and with the help of a pocket knife, cut off a chew. With the chew still against the blade and his thumb, tipped it into his mouth the same way he had done a hundred times before. He had the stains of tobacco around his mouth and whiskers and the sweet smell of the tobacco drifting towards me was like incense to a Buddhist monk. He had a twinkle in his eye

CHAPTER 8

and enjoyed the company, even from the kids who were getting rambunctious after the long trip.

He said his nephew was flying in from Montana soon with an elk he had shot and that we could all have some hearty eating for dinner. True to his word, his nephew showed up and it wasn't long afterward we were dining on the most delicious elk roast I have ever eaten, before then or since. The time we spent with Davy was unforgettable and even though it happened over forty years ago, I still recall it with clarity and deep personal affection. He gave me a plug of his tobacco and I still have it to this day. Each time I pop open the box in which I have it stashed, along with my other memorabilia, the odor plays a sweet tune in my memory. For a moment, I'm back on the porch of the log house in the Kiamichi Mountains reminiscing with the grandson of Davy Crockett himself. We spent the night and were off at first light for our next destination.

There was a small grocery store in Poteau so we figured a refill on the diapers, eats and beer were in order, especially the beer. Upon entering the store, I was surprised to find old church organs situated at each end of the aisles. They were all restored with new bellows and reeds and after a new coat of varnish and wax, they looked beautiful with their pull stops and lantern holders. They had intricately carved music stands and sometimes mirrors placed in amongst the woodwork and filigree on these genuine antiques. The proprietor of the store salvaged them from the surrounding churches when they upgraded to the electronic models and had completely refurbished them himself as a hobby. They were for sale and were averaging around $300.00 each, a price I found more than fair and I wished I had a truck I could ship these back to California on and make a nice profit.

The deeper we got into the mountains, the poorer the houses looked and it was after several hours we turned into a piece of property owned by yet another of A.C.'s kin. The house was nothing more than a tar paper shack with a dirt floor. I had never seen anything like it before. The young man and his wife were very hospitable and welcomed us in as though we were royalty. I was beginning to comprehend the Indian way of life, just a tad, and as I mingled with the Choctaw relatives of A.C. I felt the real meaning of what fellowship really is. Not the kind we know of in the so-called civilized world of exploitation and greed but a profound respect for each other as real human beings. We ate together and played together songs from long ago: Patty Page and the Sons of the Pioneers, Hank Williams, and that newcomer Johnny Cash.

We got to talk about music and guitars and I mentioned that I would dearly love to get my hands on a Doughbro guitar but knew they were like looking for hen's teeth. Ray, our host, got down on the dirt floor and reached under his bed and retrieved an old guitar. It was dark maroon in color and had a few strings missing and the metal disc was a little tarnished but by gum it was a for-real, fair-dinkum Doughbro. He wanted me to have it. Here was a couple who I had just met and he wanted me to have the only thing of value he and his wife owned. I politely refused and changed the subject to other topics less likely to cause a breach of etiquette such as the Doughbro.

Time was running out and we directed the old pick-up north towards Wichita and headed home. It was summer and the weather warm, and the kids didn't mind riding in the bed of the truck except the baby. He rode in the front with me and A.C. I asked A. C. what his name meant; what did the A and the C stand for? He

CHAPTER 8

said, "Nothin', that's how it is with some Indians." He knew of a few others with letter names that meant nothing other than what they were such as J. W. or L.C.

We got home just as the tornado warning sounded. I had never heard the siren before and thought we were in for an air raid or something. Figured the Germans were ready to reclaim some of their losses may be. We unloaded the truck and headed down into the basement. A. C. decided to run across the street and get a bucket of Kentucky Chicken before they closed and, of course, a couple of six packs of the ever present "Libation". You never knew, it might be some time before we got the "all clear". The tornado did not hit us straight on, but we did get a thunderous bout of hail and rain. The hail was about the size of golf balls and caused a ton of damage to the neighborhood around us. The new car dealers especially got it bad and they had hail sales for the next couple of weeks. The poor cars looked like the skin of a golf ball, all dinged and dimpled. Not even the best body shops in town could fix these cars without a lot of work and expense, so they were sold off at a loss if you wanted a new car with a dimpled textured finish.

I noticed an old car in A. C.'s back yard and asked him whose it was and he said it was his. It was an Oldsmobile 1956 model and other than sitting in the weeds was in pretty good shape. It was a two-door coupe with a two-tone paint job and had not run for several months. I asked him what was wrong with it and he didn't know; it just quit running. He said if I got it going I could have it and left it up to me to do with it whatever I wanted.

I checked the plugs and replaced the points and condenser. I checked the oil and filled the radiator with water. I had him pull his truck around back and give me a jump start, which he did.

The old car came to life and purred like a kitten. I now had a way home and began to get it in good enough shape for a trip to California. I charged up the battery and checked the tires for wear. They weren't great but good enough for the journey. The interior was clean and the radio even worked. The kelly green dash shone like new and the faded two-tone green and white exterior looked like it hadn't seen a wash rag in many months but after a scrub down shone pretty nice.

It was with a heavy heart I loaded up my gear and prepared to hit highway 54 to Tucumcari, New Mexico and then route 40 all the way home to Los Angeles, California. A. C. knew I liked guns and wanted me to take his old model 97 Winchester pump 12 gauge that was factory nickel plated and his pride and joy. I again had to refuse the generous offer and told him he could bring it to California sometime and give it to me then. He gave me a couple of hundred bucks to get me home and said not to worry about paying him back, ever.

I wouldn't see A.C. and the kids for some time. It wasn't in California, but in Oregon, when I was on my honeymoon, that he showed up on my front doorstep. He had the kids and a neighbor of his needing a place to stay and some hot grub. Turnabout is fair play and I was happy to get him a place to stay and a job to feed his family. We had to poach a deer or two to feed them but all in all it worked out fine.

I remember his neighbor had never seen a .44 Magnum pistol before and the one I was using to get our food was a Ruger Super Blackhawk, a new model just on the market. He wanted to shoot it so I asked if had ever shot a magnum before. He said he had and gave me the impression he was a little on the smart-aleck side and

CHAPTER 8

knew all there was to know about guns and how to shoot them. We were in the mountains and parked in a clearing looking uphill to the tree line about 300 yards away. The doors to my car were open and the three of us standing beside it scanning the hills for deer. I took the .44 and said, "Okay, now's the time you can give her a try." He took the gun and laid it on top of the car door as if it was a rifle rest and crouched down to sight through the sights. I didn't say anything but waited till he fired one off. Sure enough, the barrel flipped up and caught him square in the forehead, splitting the skin wide open and the blood started squirting like a water pistol over his shirt and shoes. I grabbed a rag from the trunk and held it over the laceration until it stopped bleeding. I was sorry for not saying anything prior to his pulling the trigger, but sometimes you just have to let nature take its course. We piled back into the car and made for home.

The neighbor was a small engine mechanic and it wasn't long before he had some old lawnmowers lined up in front of the house I had rented for them. They had a "For Sale" sign on them. He went around asking neighbors if they had old lawn mowers they no longer wanted. It was surprising how many did, and all they wanted was for someone to haul them off. He repaired them and soon had a nice little business going which helped pay the rent and also put some food on the table.

My wife was a new nurse that had just graduated and was working at the hospital in town. She was on night shift like most graduates were, and the time we spent together was short and precious. She had no problem with a bunch of strangers showing up at our front door and quickly adjusted to this new phenomena in style. It got a little crowded in the two bedroom apartment, but we managed to get a house in town and some furniture from the Good Will and they were on their own.

    Even though A.C. was not a religious man, sometimes the Bible truths apply. I believe it is in Ecclesiastes 11:1 where it states, "Cast your bread upon the waters and it shall return unto thee in many days." He did and it did.

CHAPTER 9

Guaymas was a sleepy little village in Mexico halfway to Jalisco and facing the Gulf of California. I don't know how this small village was the spot where the church conference chose to have the summer water ski and scuba camp this particular year. This camp was offered to college-age kids and catered to both the water ski crowd and the scuba divers also.

I was attending college at the time and the camp director asked me if I would drive one of the trucks down to Guaymas carrying the equipment and supplies for the outing. The truck he had in mind for transport was an old cab-over model with a V-6 engine and no air-conditioning or cruise control or any amenities for that matter. It did have a choke cable attached to the carburetor though that acted as a poor man's cruise control. You just pulled out the choke knob at the desired speed you wanted and push it back in when you wanted to turn it off. Mickey Mouse if you asked me and not too safe if something went wrong, and things always had a tendency to go wrong at the worst moment.

I helped the men load the truck mainly to make sure that it was evenly dispersed so I wouldn't have swaying problems and any items flying through the air if I had to brake in an emergency. We packed everything including the large compressor needed to fill the scuba tanks. We had wetsuits, surfboards, suitcases, duffle bag cases of food, some fresh vegetables, tables, tents, water bottles, sodas and everything imaginable kids would want on a camping trip.

Our point of departure was Glendale, California and this is where the conference headquarters were situated at the time.

This was back in the early 70's when there were student riots in Mexico and Hermosillo was the worst area affected. Unfortunately, Hermosillo was one of the towns we had to pass through prior to the beaches of Guaymas. I say beaches of Guaymas with my tongue in my cheek because there wasn't a real beach there; it was more like a cliff that went down to a strip of sand by the ocean. The time of departure came and we had to get on the road to try and make our destination before it got real late at night.

I had a girlfriend back then that I used to hang out with. She was one of the students usually called upon to help at camp in one capacity or the other. Most of our gang worked in the kitchen or as counselors to the younger kids. Debby was a boisterous type and was heard mostly before she was seen. Her hearty laugh and rash voice were readily distinguishable as Deb's. She wanted to ride along in the box van with me, and I could use the company as the trip was going to be long and arduous.

I had driven south of the border before and there were a few things you needed to take along to ease the tensions that sometimes presented themselves at the all too many checkpoints along the way. Now the church group I was representing was pretty staunch in their beliefs mainly regarding the various vices that most people take for granted. Right at the top of the list was drinking alcohol and the next was smoking of any kind. The trouble was the border guards didn't know the fundamental religious beliefs of the owners of the truck I was driving. A couple of packs of cigarettes go a long way in smoothing out the rough spots that occur at these routine checks. I figured what the powers that be don't know won't hurt them, or me, and consequently the trip down was uneventful.

CHAPTER 9

The students at Hermosillo were kind enough to not riot or demonstrate the time we passed through town. We set up camp and unloaded the truck as soon as we arrived. We were one of the first vehicles to come and I wondered why the rest of the caravan was taking so long. I was one of the last ones to leave and now one of the first to arrive. Then it struck me. The cigarettes.

There were about ten to twelve scuba divers and they wanted to get in the water first thing in the morning so I had to make sure their tanks were full and their equipment available and ready to go. I couldn't understand why these guys were so gung-ho about spearfishing since they were all vegetarians and didn't eat the fish they speared.

There were two ski boats that were available. One was a high sided tri-hull that was a pain in the rear to get in and out of. It did have a swim step on the rear transom, and if you couldn't climb it, you got to swim to shore to get out. The other was a low-profile day cruiser that everyone wanted to ski behind, mainly due to its ease of operation. Thank goodness the movie "Jaws" hadn't come out yet because if it had, there would be no skiing or scuba diving, period, since we were in some of the worst shark-infested waters known. I guess ignorance really is bliss.

The driver of the sleek ski boat had his hands full and the other driver, me, had no problems at all. The group I was catering to were the most experienced skiers that appreciated the outboard motor which gave a more distinctive snap to its mode of operation. The hotshot boat had a jet drive which had a longer period of drag and this caused a slower lift off on the deep water starts. We skied from sun-up to noon and finally pulled the boats in so we could break for lunch.

The frogmen returned with a bunch of beautiful red snapper. There were about twelve to fifteen of them and they were each about 20 to 24 inches long and weighed in around 6 or 7 pounds each. I am no fish expert, but these were beautiful specimens and I didn't want to see them wasted. I asked the guys if I could have them since they were showing them off. There was no resistance so I snagged them.

I lugged them up to the little shanty town about 100 yards from our camp. Poorer people you haven't seen and their shacks were constructed of cardboard from old boxes. I saw a couple of ladies and called out in my pathetic Spanish, "Hola, Senora. Como Esta?" I flagged them down and asked them to please cook the fish for me. I negotiated a price, around $5.00 if my memory serves me right, and they set to work cleaning them and preparing them for cooking. I sat and watched them salt and squeeze lime juice over them as well as adding other herbs and spices. They wrapped each one in tin foil and cooked them over a 55-gallon drum which was a makeshift oven. It didn't take more than a few minutes to have them done to perfection. I peeled the foil back on one of the fish and dug in. These women knew how to cook fish. You would think they lived by the ocean or something. They stood there looking at me as if to say, "Are you going to eat all of these fish yourself?" I laughed out loud as I read their thoughts and motioned them to help themselves. Their eyes widened and a smile spread across their faces as they each grabbed a fish. I asked if they had any "Ninos" and they both nodded. I said, "Venga Aqui, Nino e ninas, muhere," which was probably saying something out of context. I did get the point over because it wasn't too long that we had a real "fiesta". The fish were definitely put to good use. We all had our fill

CHAPTER 9

and I was reminded of the Sermon on the Mount where several thousand were fed some fishes and loaves. We had some fishes and tortillas and the good Lord to thank for them both. I made some friends that day and will always treasure the experience.

One of the kitchen helpers for the camp was a South American girl named Irma. She was about my age and had the most fantastic complexion I had ever seen. You have heard the saying about peaches and cream skin; well she had it and was a genuine beautiful girl in many ways. Being in Mexico with a person who spoke the lingo was a real plus. We became friends and spent a lot of off time together.

Debby was a bit miffed but since we weren't really going steady, she didn't actually have the right to get mad. The trip was pretty uneventful up to this point and the time came for us to pack up and start for home. I got the box truck filled and was ready to depart. Irma asked if she could ride along in the truck with Deb and I. I said, "Sure, the front seat is wide enough to fit the three of us comfortably." I don't think Deb was too crazy about the new seating arrangements, but that didn't matter much since they were friends and co-workers from the kitchen gang.

We gassed up at the first station we passed. After some time on the road, we kind of leaned back into a comfortable pace with the "speed control" pulled out and the speedometer reading around sixty mph. The roads were pretty good with excellent pavement and few pot holes. The only real problem I hated were the small bridges crossing the culverts installed for water control over which we would pass about every ten miles or so. These culverts were narrow; I mean they were almost half the width of the actual road. We would be cruising along a nice wide highway and then it would bottleneck down to half size and two seconds later we were back on the broad road once more. It was disinclining. I was being lulled into a rhythm as we flogged down the irregular strip of highway.

Irma was sitting next to me and putting pressure on my thigh with hers and leaning into my right shoulder with her left. I wasn't complaining and similar messages were being returned with gusto. In the distance, I spotted the lights of a semi truck approaching at a fast rate. As it approached, I just managed to locate a damn cul-de-sac which would put us at the crossing simultaneously. There was no way two trucks would fit on the crossings at the same time. I instinctively slammed my hand on the choke "cruise control" and inadvertently bent the friggin thing instead of pushing it in. I hit the clutch with my left foot which revved the engine to about a million rpm. I could see the other drivers face as he passed me as clearly as if I was looking into a mirror. His eyes were the size of saucers and his mouth was wide open in an inaudible scream. We didn't touch each other and to this day I call it a miracle. I grabbed the knob and tried to straighten the shaft so I could push it back in and get the engine down to a mere thousand rpm rather than the ballistic phase it was now in. Too late, the audible knock, knock, knock was already playing the rod knock anthem. Deb and Irma were both sitting there white as ghosts, peaches and cream and all else, out the window. It was a minute or two before anyone spoke. Deb, who was never at a loss for words, just muttered "Di- did, did you see that?" I swear I felt the seat get warm and wet at the same time but upon checking was mistaken. I wouldn't blame Irma if she had because I was close to doing it myself. Here we were in the middle of Mexico with a rod knocking and a long way home. What now?

CHAPTER 9

Even though the truck was banging away it was still drivable. I had to keep it under 25mph or it wrapped too loud and felt like it was going to explode. We crippled into Hermosillo just as the student riots were at their peak. There were school buses lying on their sides on fire and rocks and garbage strewn all over the streets. The crowd was on the other side of town and I was glad of it. Our decrepit box van limped to a safe zone where I could do some work on it. We parked under a tree at the edge of town and I left Deb with the van to keep an eye on it while Irma and I looked for an auto parts store to get some items. I was glad Irma was with us at that moment so she could help me get the parts I needed to patch up the engine enough to get us home. We found a store and I told Irma that I needed just one set of standard connecting rod bearings for the model truck we had and the year. I also needed some oil and a pan gasket. I didn't realize that there was such a difference in the Spanish language from one country to the other. Apparently Irma was from Guatemala, and trying to explain to a Mexican about items she had no concept of was beginning to get comical if it wasn't such a dangerous a situation. She would rattle on in Spanish and the proprietor would shake his head and go, "Que?" She would begin again and then the "Que?" would follow. This kept up for some time until I asked her if she was talking Spanish or maybe Portuguese. "Que?" she said and burst out laughing.

Finally, we had what we needed and carried our stuff back to the truck. Luckily there were a few tools in the back of the truck and I managed to drop the pan and inspect the loose rod. Putting the new bearing insert in wasn't going to solve the problem but it might help it enough get us home. I filed the insert ends down even smaller than the standard size and reinstalled the rod cap.

I changed the oil to the thickest possible; I think 50 weight, and started it up. The noise was at least 75% better than it was before, and we could now cruise along at thirty-five to forty miles per hour.

It was now the middle of the night and I was super tired. This last escapade had taken its toll on all of us and we needed to get some sleep. We opened the back of the box van and spread out the surfboards and anything flat to form a bed of some sort. There were sleeping bags the students were sending home with us and we opened them up and spread them out on the makeshift bed. We crawled in and snuggled down into the downy mattress. Deb was on my left and Irma on my right. Under these circumstances, I couldn't drop off to sleep. Irma was holding my right hand and Deb my left and I was playing Romeo to both of them at the same time unbeknown to them.

At some point, we all fell asleep and upon awaking early the next morning the hand playing restarted. Finally I faked arising, sat up and yawned, and said we must hit the road if we were to get back by the weekend. We piled in the front seat and after they had figured who was to sit next to me for the next leg of the journey, we left. The girls had it figured that each time we stopped for gas they switched places. This worked out well and the ride home was pretty nice until we reached Los Angeles.

Driving slow in Mexico was fine because most of the people drove that way and we melded right in, but here in L.A. it was different. Driving at thirty-five mph on the freeways was not fun. The knocking got worse and the engine started to smoke a bit. I was surprised the police didn't pull me over for holding up traffic, but they didn't. I crawled into the conference parking lot late that evening and was rewarded for my diligent effort of getting the

CHAPTER 9

stuff home with a reprimand for taking so long getting back. Like the old adage goes, "no good deed will go unpunished". The time with Irma and Deb will remain with me forever as a definite "high" in my life and the experience in Mexico was priceless.

CHAPTER 10

Guns have always been a source of wonderment and awe for me, ever since I was a kid. I think it stems from all the western movies I watched as a juvenile. I was raised in New Zealand, but the movies I had at the weekend cinema were Tom Mix, Roy Rogers, Gene Autry or some other super cowboy that my friends and I identified with.

My mother couldn't afford the cowboy outfit I dreamed of in the Sears catalog we had, but she created a fantastic outfit of her own and with a little imagination and a sewing machine she created miracles. I remember my chaps were made from gunny sacks, but the fringes down the sides might as well as been rawhide from the delight it gave me. My checkered shirt was with a solid-colored yoke and an edge dividing the top from the bottom. She didn't have snap-on buttons but never mind, no one else had them yet either.

It didn't help that my older brother was into guns also. After we had migrated to the United States and after my brother did his stint in the U.S. Navy, he purchased a .357 Magnum pistol from Ruger Arms. I was 13 at the time and pretty adventurous kid for my age.

Not far from my home was a drive-in theater called the "Rhodium". To offset their slow periods they used to hold a swap meet on the weekends to supplement their income. It only cost a dollar to get in, and the vendors paid a minimal amount to sell their goods. Those were the good old days when you could buy and sell anything. There was an old man that always had several guns for sale there, and I would manage to pick up one once in a while if it were cheap enough. I couldn't afford a pistol, but I did buy some shotguns and rifles. One of the shotguns I bought was an antique double-barreled 12 gauge. It was constructed with Damascus steel and had exposed hammers. You flipped the lever and broke the rifle in two so you could insert the shells, and then flip the barrels up and you were ready to fire. The barrels were a little rusty and the engraving down the obliterated barrels was endured over the years.

    I had no idea that you should only shoot low-grade ammo in such an old firearm. I managed to acquire a box of 12 gauge magnum double buckshot rounds. To prove that fools rush in where angels fear to tread, I opened up the cartridge shot cavity and filled it with liquid paraffin. Some expert told me that this would hold the shot together longer and give a closer shot pattern. I didn't know what a shot pattern was but figured it would blow a bigger hole in whatever I was shooting. I thank the good Lord that Damascus steel was as sturdy as it was because I shot holes in old junk cars and 3/4-inch plywood scrap big enough to stuff a cat through. It was another real miracle that the gun didn't blow up in my face. I had shot many boxes of ammo through it before I sold it to one of my friends.

Another thing that happened to me back in those formative years, to show how ignorant kids can be, that could have turned into a real tragedy. Steve lived two streets over from mine and we shared the eighth grade together. He was a little on the wild side, and this made him interesting to be around. Steve was a rare case since he was one of the few kids in school from a broken home. He lived with his mother and seldom saw his dad, which I think was fine with him. Divorce was not commonly known and in my class of thirty or more kids, only two were from divorced parents. Today

CHAPTER 10

that statistic is pretty much reversed. His mother was Cuban and his dad a slick operator from Vegas or Reno. I met him once or twice and thought he came from a movie set. His black hair was slicked down, and he sported a thin mustache like the gangsters used to wear. He always wore open neck sports shirts with a blazer, black slacks and those brogue shoes with white saddles across the tops of them and shoelaces with little leather tufts on the ends. He constantly had a cigarette in his mouth and smelled like Old Spice cologne. Steve's mom was a waitress and used to come home at night, when we would help her count out her tip money. She would dump it on the table and head for the bath. She complained about her legs and feet aching all the time. I guess being a waitress must suck because she made no secret of how it affected her physical being. It paid well because we would count out about $300.00 a night in tips, and that was in 1959, and wasn't including her salary. She was a beautiful woman, and I'm sure this was a contributing factor to her tip money.

It was late afternoon when I arrived at Steve's place, and he was in his garage messing around with a box full of stuff he had in front of him. He had an old coin collection with silver dollars and half dollars, all kinds of silver coins, and all in books that held particular years in sets. He also had a couple of automatic pistols. One was a military .45 Colt and the other a .32 Beretta. Both were loaded, and both looked very imposing. I didn't ask him where he got them, but I did look them over. We dropped the clips out of them so we wouldn't accidently shoot someone. To a thirteen-year-old kid, holding a .45 was like holding absolute power in the palm of your hand. It got a little giddy there for a moment with Steve holding the .32 and me the .45. We started doing stupid things like whipping around in a fast draw move aping John Wayne in one of his WWII war classics. Then we got real crazy and held the gun to our heads and went, "kapow", and faked a head shot and flung our heads back like we had pulled the trigger.

After all this foolishness, I pointed the gun towards the back of the garage and as an afterthought pulled the trigger. BAM, the thing fired and put a hole through the rear wall. There was a bullet in the chamber we failed to eject. We just stood there and looked at each other for a second, I got weak in the knees, and the gun just hung there by my side still smoking from the explosion. We heard screaming coming from inside the house, and we ran inside after hiding the weapons. Steve's mom was in the bathroom, and she stood there wrapped in a towel and pointing to a large hole in the wall between the faucet handles and said, "What happened?" Steve told her we were playing with some ammunition in the garage, and we dropped around on the floor and it went off and shot through the wall. Any man would have known the stupidity of that statement but with his mom we got away with it. The bullet had penetrated the back wall of the garage which abutted the bathroom. It then went through the tiles on the wall and went through the back wall of the bathroom about six inches above the lip of the tub. It went into Steve's room and through the rear of his dresser and was lying in his underwear in the second draw down. If I had shot the gun two or three seconds later, I would have killed his mom. She was about to step into the tub when this all occurred. To this day, I cringe as I write this because of what could have happened thirty years ago. Steve had to face his dad about this whole affair. I was glad I wasn't there when that transpired because he wouldn't buy the cartridge thing, and Steve would have to concoct something believable or else.

CHAPTER 10

You would think we would have learned our lesson from the gun incident, but gun powder and mischief are too tempting for teenagers, and so it wasn't long before we were neck deep in it again. This time we were not playing with guns but with bombs. It started out innocently enough with us building rockets out of used up CO_2 cartridges. These cartridges were used in BB guns to propel the BB's out the barrel. When they are empty, you just discard them. We came up with the great idea of stuffing the empty cylinder with match heads and igniting them and watching them shoot across the field. They would explode like a firecracker and fly about 100 to 150 yards away. We got inspired and decided to solder fins on the sides of the cartridge and make it more like a rocket. We did, and it worked so well we had to paint the thing with bright nail polish so we could retrieve it easier. Sometimes they flew and sometimes they blew up. There was no way of anticipating which was about to happen, so we always prepared for the worst and put a cinder block on each side of it before setting it off.

Over the weeks, the ridiculous turned into the sublime. We had graduated from the CO_2 cylinders to full on pipe bombs. I figured out this on my own, and it surprised me to find out over the years that other people had figured out the same method and called them pipe bombs. Our enthusiasm culminated in one last hurrah and after all the smaller bombs we had finally arrived at a two and a half inch x eight-inch "killer". To fill it with match heads we had to get cartons of book matches and sit there with tin snips and cut the heads off each book with one fell swoop. It took several cartons to fill the thing, and of course we had to make enough to form a fuse long enough for us to get away.

We had reverted to shoplifting to afford the things necessary to complete the "killer". We were now entering the criminal world, and I knew if this continued I would be in real trouble. I was a churchgoer from very young, and my conscience was beginning to bother me actually. I knew this was the last time I would do anything so malevolent. Finally, it was finished and the only thing left to do was to set it off. We had found a field right across from the firehouse that had a pile of old sidewalk slabs piled up from some road construction going on down the street. We placed the bomb under some of the slabs and ran a two-foot fuse from the hole at the end of the cap through a trough in the sandy soil to a safe place to light it. I lit the fuse, and we ran to the street about fifty yards away. The explosion was deafening. An enormous red flash flew up and out, and the entire field was instantly on fire. This field was about three building sections long and like half an acre. We stood there dumbfounded, until a woman started yelling, "It's those boys over there, the one in the red shirt, and the other one." She had been hanging up her washing in her back yard when all this happened.

Sirens started wailing almost immediately, not from across the street but down the road and we figured it was the police. We ran like the devil himself was after us and I took off my shirt and stuffed it in a hedge as we went. "Stupid" doesn't come close to describing the antics I got myself into, and looking back I can only say only through the grace of God did I survive. I'm sure this chapter won't be published, but it will be a personal section I will keep for posterity.

CHAPTER 11

"Spring has sprung and fall has fell, summers here and it's ... hotter'n it was last year." Jim was always quoting poetry albeit his version usually was some other cockeyed rendition from the far side. His greatest fountain of wealth was the "Mad Magazine" to which he was a devout fan. He thoroughly memorized the Mad Magazine's version of "The Raven" by Edgar Allen Poe. To this day, he can rattle it off verbatim.

Spring had sprung and the weather was marvelous. Jim and I drove up to the dairy to see Tom about something and as we pulled up in our trusty Jeep, I noticed some of the herds were exercising their right to play-act their fantasies. The cows were humping each other, so I said to Jim, "Do you think we ought to spoil their fun and tell them it ain't no bull on top?"

About that time Tom walked up and said "Hi."

Jim said, "Tom, your cows are getting a little frisky with each other, reckon it's because it's springtime in the Rockies?"

Tom laughed and told us it was their usual behavior when the cows came into heat; they accommodated each other with a little role play. He mentioned that he needed to get them fertilized so his milk production wouldn't suffer. He had a new bull he wanted to try out, but he wasn't too sure of his track record since he didn't even have one yet. He was going to start tomorrow and could use a hand or two with getting things started. We said we would be available and would be there the following morning.

The fact was you couldn't keep us back with something as intriguing as this. We were going to assist "Ajax" in his God-given right to procreation. I told Jim if he knew what was in store for him on the morrow he probably wouldn't get any sleep tonight.

Roland Johanssen worked at the dairy and was a unique individual since he believed he was a direct descendant of Eric the Red or some other Viking superhero. He was utterly fearless and because of his archaic beliefs he was a loose cannon in many ways. He wouldn't hesitate a split second at a dare to do anything outlandish or dangerous. I remember one time a classmate dared him to throw a rock through the principal's office window and before you could say "stop", it was done. Ten kids were running in every direction to absent themselves from Roland and the impending disaster to soon follow. How he stayed in school was to most a mystery. I knew his father was a prominent contractor who built condos in Newport Beach and I wondered how much it cost him to keep Roland in school and off the streets.

The fateful day arrived and as soon as we finished breakfast we were in the Jeep headed straight for the dairy. Tom was already in the pen with our lucky cow, soon to be mated with our illustrious Ajax, the progenitor. I asked Tom what her name was, thought I would try and get this on a more personable basis, and he said, "Slewfoot Sue." She had a bad habit of turning around and staring at you as you tried to herd her in for milking. Tom was a bit of a greenhorn when it came to this mating business and was a little leery about the whole affair since the school dropped "Animal Husbandry." He said, "Hell, it's just animal nature, it can't be too difficult, eh?" I caught a bit of Canada there with the "eh?" Somehow when one gets a bit nervous ones, heritage floats to the surface. I could see why the nervous part came into play when Tom opened the adjoining gate and Ajax came prancing in the arena. He

CHAPTER 11

knew something was up the way he flung his head high and snorted a few times. He curled his upper lip in an unmistakable gesture of excitement and zeroed in on poor Slewfoot Sue.

Now the word had leaked out in the boys dorm that some sort of sexual education proceedings were going on at the dairy and half dozen looky-loos showed up for a little excitement. They positioned themselves around the top rung of the pen where the actual deed was to be performed and eagerly watched for the event to begin.

Ajax, now thoroughly aroused, strutted around the pen stopping only once in a while to sniff the back end of Sue, further inflaming his passion and drive. The snot began to run as Ajax pranced around and as he flung his massive head about, the mucous stream flew over the boys on the top rung, not in the least dampening their transfixed ogling. They were too intent on their cheering capabilities to notice such a small thing as bull snot dripping off their shirts and britches. "Go get her Ajax," they screamed. "Right on, buddy," they hollered as if they were chanting for themselves in some way or another.

Ajax, not at all stifled by the instant fame hurled at him from the peanut gallery, finally stopped his pacing and walked up to Slewfoot's rear and after a few more sniffs tried to mount her. Being a newcomer to this whole mating thing, he was seemingly learning as he went. He had the equipment and he knew which end it was supposed to enter, the problem was he couldn't seem to actually get it together. He managed a few misses, leaving a stream of sperm over the side of Sue, but couldn't seem to hit a home run, if you catch my drift? The more the boys urged him on and the poorer Ajax failed, the more frustrated Tom got. He said he was afraid something like this would happen with a bull like this. I said, "All he needed was a little help that's all. If you could get someone to guide him in where he needed to be, it would be okay. Tom looked at me as if to say, "Who the hell would be stupid enough to do ..." Just then he yelled, "Roland, get over here, I gotta job for you."

Roland came running from inside the milking shed with his rubber boots flapping each other as he ran. "What's up boss?" he said. It's the first time Roland hesitated doing anything. The thought of him jumping in there with a two-ton bull trying to do what he wants to do but can't, didn't appeal to Roland in any way. The confused look still is implanted in my mind as I recollect the moment in time. Unfortunately, there was an audience and Roland's Viking pride could not be questioned here. He slowly walked toward Ajax as he was still doing his damnedest to get things done. Apparently Roland approached him from the blind side and he wasn't noticed until he grabbed the misguided missile with his right hand. Ajax stopped midstream what he was doing and froze for a second. His eyes rolled back in his head and he let out a bellow that literally shook the ground. The cheering section jumped off the top rung and fled. Jim and I were transfixed as Tom yelled out, "Now stuff it in her, man." I could literally see the hair on the back of Roland's neck stand up on end and I firmly believed he thought this was going to be the last day of his life. "Stuff it in yourself," he yelled as he made a mad dash for the gate.

I think he finally met his match when it came to being a daredevil. Slewfoot Sue just turned around and glared, as usual, as if to add "What's all the fuss?" Ajax, finally worn out from his amorous encounter, stood motionless in the middle of the pen, well spent from his misadventure at lovemaking. "Well the day's

CHAPTER 11

not a total waste," Tom added, "I can take some sperm samples off the side of Slew and see how prolific our lover boy could be. Never know, he might be shooting blanks. We will give it another go tomorrow and maybe have a better day of it."

I said, "I don't think Roland will be too eager to participate a second time, and if it wasn't for the onlookers he probably wouldn't have done it the first time."

Tom replied, "Let's just hope for the best and chalk this episode up to first-time jitters." Slewfoot, still in hearing range turned around once more and glared again as if to say, "Bring him on."

CHAPTER 12

Las Vegas has always held a particular fascination for not only me but all my friends at school. We would gather in someone's room and eventually the talk would evolve to the big lights and fancy casinos. It wasn't until one of them came up with a foolproof system of betting that we began to plan a trip to the city of lights to try it out. I don't know exactly where this system came from, but we tried it out with match sticks and a worn out deck of cards, and it seemed to pay off even after weeks of practice. The system was a simple one and consisted of putting down on paper 1121 which was the sequence of bets. First you bet the one in front, then if you won, you bet the second one, and if you won that, you bet the two, etc. The thing was that if you lost, you doubled up your bets until you won and then carried on with the sequence.

I remember running back to the room after classes and pulling out the deck and with someone dealing the cards, we would play Black Jack till late at night and we always came out winners. You seldom lost more than five or six in a row, so the doubling up of your bets didn't get out of hand. It wouldn't take long for your kitty to go bust if you lost on the two, and if you went six straight losses, you had to recoup. That would run up to a hundred twenty-eight dollar bet. I wasn't the only one doing the math on this system; a few of my friends were becoming card sharks too, and we were all winning. I couldn't figure out how come someone hadn't thought of this before now and was already making a killing in Vegas already. That was their terrible luck 'cause we were going to bust the bank, and with all the practice and rehearsals we had invested, we couldn't lose.

The six weeks leave was fast approaching and us at the Academy were ready for it. We had amassed our fortunes by cashing in all the scrap metal we could scrounge up around the school and workshops and selling it to the metal merchants in town. Truckloads of metal, consisting of lead, aluminum, cast iron and scrap tin and whatever, we hauled onto the scales to be weighed and cashed in our metal. Some of the items we pulled were questionable as to their designation of "scrap" but we couldn't be fussy; we had a mission, and we were going to give it our best shot.

The school owned an old Ford pick-up that had only one door on the passenger side. It was a 1942 model, and the reason the door was missing was to let the driver jump in and out of it quickly when picking up trash around the school campus. The school had graduated to a regular trash truck, and the old Ford retired to the farm shop. We had full use of the old truck, and it came in handy when we hauled the metal to the scrap yard to sell. Driving down the freeway without a door was a little unnerving, but necessary to reach our goal. I did a few tune-ups at the garage, on the side after hours, to make some extra cash, and Jim sold some oranges off the ranch where he lived to pocket a couple extra bucks.

We drove the old Ford over the back roads starting in Newbury Park all the way to Santa Paula, where Jim lived and got a few cases of oranges to bring back to the school to sell. We all couldn't fit in the front, so Wayne and Bud sat in the back while we hot-footed it over the mountain range separating the two destinations. The main canyon we finally had to drive through was called Lambs Canyon, and it was steep and narrow and not a few cars had gone over the side into the abysmal canyon below. There were always a couple of California condors flying over that area, and it added

CHAPTER 12

to the foreboding mood it caused as we descended. I put the old Ford in second gear, and we started down. You could see over the side the carcasses of the many cars and trucks that hadn't made it through and it did give you a feeling of wonderment as to their fate. Some of the vehicles were the result of kids stealing them and shoving them over to witness the carnage as the cars flipped over and over on their way down the cliff. The others I can only guess as to their particular tale of woe.

We made it down and headed to the ranch. Jim's mom was special, always with a smile and some quirky saying that usually fit the situation to a tee. When we arrived on her doorstep she said, "I would say 'look what the cat dragged in' but my cat has better manners." She was a fantastic cook and on many occasions she brought to our dorm room a cobbler of some kind or another; whether it be a blackberry one or an apricot one, it all tasted terrific. One time she brought Jim an apricot cobbler and left it in the room for us boys, and before Jim got out of class, I had cleaned up the whole thing myself. He never really forgave me for that one but understood how I could do it: she was a fantastic cook. We all came in and visited for a while and of course she fed us a great meal before we headed to the backyard to fill a few cases with oranges to take back to school.

The academy had a "Cash and Carry" along the highway that sold gasoline and other products at the school. There were the eggs and the milk and always fresh pastries the school imported from a bakery in town. We figured that we could add a case or two of oranges from the ranch to sell also, either a case at a time or by the pound. It wasn't long before we had amassed a small fortune between us, and we were ready for the big event.

We decided to drive Bud's Chevelle to Vegas because we could all fit in comfortably, and it was one of the most reliable vehicles between us. The day came, and we all piled in and headed down Highway 101 to Los Angeles, and then 10 to the 215 and north to Lost Wages. It took us about four hours to drive there and the excitement cooped up in that two-door coupe was explosive to say the least. We all had complete faith in "The System" because it had worked hundreds of times in our practice sessions and the odds, we were certain, were in our favor.

It took forever but finally the lights of Vegas were in the distance. As we descended from the mountain and hit the straight-a-way that shot you directly into town, we all gave a "whoop" to take the pressure off a tad. It was 1963 and the scene before us was different than today. There were no mega casinos with pirate ships and huge lions out front. The two prominent casinos at that time were Caesar's Palace and Circus Circus down the street. The Horseshoe and Thunderbird were still there and also the Frontier and Harrah's. Main Street, or the "Old Town", was still the big attraction and drew the most people en-masse to the open streets and bright lights. It was truly amazing, and the sheer extravaganza of the entire scene was overwhelming.

We each had a pocket full of cash, and we were ready for action. None of us was twenty-one, but we were big for our age. In those days, they weren't as picky whose money they took. We decided to split up and do our thing and meet back at the Denny's restaurant, our designated spot, around one in the morning. Everything was pretty much within walking distance so getting around was no problem. I set my sights on Caesar's Palace and strode in.

Now this system of ours would work in most situations or

CHAPTER 12

games, but we figured that playing "red" or "black" on the roulette wheel was as good as any. I decided to start with Black Jack and shift to the roulette wheel later in the evening. I found a dollar table with a cute girl working it and sat down, reached into my wallet and produced a hundred dollar bill and asked for some chips. The dealer looked at me a little strange when I procured a small pad of paper and a pen from my pocket wrote down 1121 on the top and placed a bet. I lucked out and got a king and an ace for blackjack and after crossing off the first 1, bet another dollar. Everything went as planned and I began to amass a small pile of chips in front of me, which drew an interest from the looky loos walking the floors but never indulging on their own. The curious smile the dealer had grown into a more inquisitive gesture as time wore on, and she finally asked me what I was up to. I naively stated that it was a system my buddies, and I learned, and we were all giving it a try this weekend. By this time I had acquired about twelve hundred dollars and the gang around me increased also. They were intent on figuring out my system and kept looking over my shoulder as I crossed off the numbers on the top and then rewriting them down lower on the page and then starting all again.

I couldn't believe my luck as the system kept working, as I kept betting, and the pile grew. I remember a cocktail girl coming by every hour or two and asking me if I wanted a drink on the house. I kept refusing because I didn't like the taste of booze, but she kept trying over and over again. I didn't mind. She was cute, and the outfit she was wearing didn't leave a lot to the imagination, and the Coke or Pepsi I did get periodically gave her a tip or two to add to her purse.

They changed dealers on me, and I was sorry to see my smiling cohort leave, but I doggedly continued till I had about two grand in front of me. It was pushing one o'clock, and I was to meet the other guys at Denny's soon, so I decided to cash in my chips and leave. I had a pocket full of money, and I was flush with excitement.

I walked to Denny's and entered the front door. My buddies weren't there yet, so I stood in line for a table. Around the lobby of the restaurant were a dozen or so slot machines. A few patrons stagnated the room pulling the handles looking for the elusive jackpot. I asked the person behind me if he wouldn't mind holding my place in line while I gave it a go at the slots. He agreed, and I walked to the first machine and inserted a dollar slug. I pulled the handle and watched the wheels spin: "Ka-plunk" a gold nugget, "ka-plunk" a gold nugget, and "ka-plunk", another gold nugget.

The bells went ""ding-ding-ding" and the whistles blew as three hundred and twenty bucks spilled into the tin tray in front of me. A few people gave a cheer as I got a bucket and scooped up my loot.

I returned to my place in line as my friends walked in the door. It wasn't long before we got a table, and we all sat around swapping stories about our different escapades. I said I was treating dinner because I had just hit a jackpot two minutes before they got there, and I was hot. Some of the stories weren't good, and somehow they had lost most of their seed money. I said I was doing great, and they couldn't believe my luck. I showed them my twenty-one hundred dollar bills and the bucket of slots at the table, and they stared in disbelief. They decided to keep the money they had left and check out the girls in town.

I returned to the Palace and was going to break the bank. I decided to try the roulette wheel and play the "red" in hopes

CHAPTER 12

for another run of luck like before. It was late, and the crowds were thinning out a bit but it was Vegas and it never actually sleeps. I found the table and started to make my bets. I did alright and settled in for some action. The notepad brought the usual response, but I didn't care; I just kept on betting and scribbling, betting and scribbling.

Now the thing with the system was you had to stick with it no matter what. If you lost faith in its magic, you lost everything. It was getting to be four o'clock in the morning, and I had made a few dollars but not like before, and I was getting tired. The ever-present cocktail girls kept coming by and finally I said, "Do you know what I would like?" After a short while with no guess, and an expression I can only compare to as a deer in the headlights look, I said, "An excellent cigar." I had this weird idea that a cigar might keep me awake if I could puff on it once in a while for enjoyment. She took off like a shot and was back with a silver tin container with an excellent cigar inside, wrapped in a sheet of cedar wood paper batting and smelling like a million. I lit it up and sucked in a mouthful of smoke. It was wonderful. I have never smoked a cigar as delicious as that one. Of course, I have only smoked about five in the last forty years but that was the absolute best. I wish I had the forethought of writing down the name of it, heck I even had a pen and paper, but I didn't. I smoked it entirely down to the nubbin.

My luck began to turn, and I was getting a little nervous about its validity. I ran into a streak of atrocious turns, that to this day rings of wheel manipulation or some other form of mechanical wizardry. I lost ten straight times on a two dollar bet, and that constitutes a two thousand and forty-eight dollar bet. I figured I was going to stick with the system and bet it. I can still remember the little white ball bobbing around as the wheel spinned. "Ka-plunk", it fell into the black one more time and cleaned me out. I walked away from the table and didn't hear the, "Sorry, sir" or "Tough luck man" echoing away in some lost corner of my mind.

I had won a bundle and lost a bundle, all in the space of a few hours in the vast city of gamblers, Las Vegas. I sat in the main lobby for a while licking my wounds and contemplating how I was going to pass this piece of news on to the other guys. I must have been a pitiful sight sitting there when a beautiful woman walked up to me and spoke. She dressed in some fine clothes and looked every inch a professional model. Her hair was brunette, and the fur around her shoulders made from mink. She had on an evening gown, black, with diamonds sewn in the fabric to sparkle as the lights from the Marquis hit them and reflected all around. She looked like Tina Louise the actress, which most guys my age swooned over whenever her image hit the screen, or they had posters of her on their dorm room walls. She had on stiletto heeled shoes that brought out the curves in her legs and thighs, which were evident through the slit in her dress all the way up to her right hip. She had the mole on her face too, just like Tina, only in a different spot.

She was gorgeous and made me melt right down to my shoes. She rendered me speechless for a moment. She said, "Do you want to spend some time with me tonight?" I realized she was a high-class hooker, and I couldn't afford five minutes with her at this point. It was a blessing I had lost all my money because who knows what kind of life I might have fallen into if I hadn't. I looked up into those hazel brown eyes and said, "If only I hadn't lost all my money at roulette twenty minutes ago." Her smile turned into a mock look of despair with her lips pursed, and her eyebrows knitted in an, "I wish you hadn't either boy". The whole affair lasted less than five minutes, but it is like indelible ink on my mind and will be there until I die. There was only one other woman who affected me the same way as this Tina look-a-like, and it was the first time I laid eyes on my second wife some twenty years later.

I gathered my wits about me and faced the door. I shoved it open and stepped out into the desert night. I learned a great lesson that night, and it has stuck with me through the years. I asked myself, "Who pays for all those crystal chandeliers hanging in the casinos?" The answer is always the same: "Idiots like you who think they can beat the bank." The trip back was less noisy and the sullen looks on the guys faces showed that no one came out ahead. We did have some fun, and we did learn some valuable lessons that I think stuck with most of us. None of us ever became professional gamblers and probably never will be.

CHAPTER 13

La Rumorosa is a small dot on the desert road between Tijuana and Mexicali just south of the USA and Mexican border. I had never heard of this place before until talking to a pal of mine affectionately called Primo, which is cousin in Spanish. He told me about a couple of gold miners who lived just south of La Rumorosa where they had staked a claim and were working the claim with ancient equipment and needed help. I agreed to go down there and look the place over and see what I could do for them in exchange for a share in the mine.

It was around 1975 or so and I was director of engineering at a large hospital in Los Angeles. East L.A. was predominately Mexican Americans at that time so I had many dealings with Mexicans and I also had a few working for me as well. Primo was my all-round construction man who would do any job from setting the tile and pouring cement to hanging dropped ceilings as well as stud and sheetrock work. He did all with expert craftsmanship and I relied on him heavily for all phases of work. We became close friends and I ate at his house many times, and not just because his wife's cooking was superb. She did everything the old-world way which just made everything taste so much better. I found their company refreshing and fulfilling. His wife had just had a baby and he was trying to think of a name for him. I said Primo, your last name is Ramirez, why don't you call him Raul, and it rhymes with Ramirez nicely."

He thought for a moment and said, "Yes, that is a respectable name, Raul Ramirez." That is his name today and a beautiful boy he turned out to be.

We chose a time to go down south and loaded up my Chevy pickup and took off. It would take us about three and a half to four hours to reach our goal and I wanted to make sure we had plenty of food and water from the states to hold us over for the weekend. I had heard the horror stories of Montezuma's revenge from drinking the water there and eating unwashed foods; I didn't want any of it. Our route would take us through Tijuana and then head due east to La Rumorosa. We planned on stopping at Tijuana (TJ) to see the sights and pick up some trinkets. I wanted some leather goods and there were some good buys there.

Crossing the border always filled me with trepidation knowing I didn't have the protection of Uncle Sam any longer until I returned. There were horror stories about wrongful arrests and just plain murder for whatever you had on you. I had to knock off this attitude and enjoy the trip for what it was. It was a hot day and going through the desert would be grueling at 120 degrees plus, with no air-conditioning.

We parked just off Revolution Boulevard, the main drag through TJ, and began our shopping spree in town. Primo wanted to get some items for his kids and I headed for the leather merchants. There were things there you couldn't find in L.A. such as chaps of all kinds, shotgun and open back ones, and leather gloves with gauntlets. There was an array of belts and buckles too that caught your eye right off. Some had silver studs and Mexican coins embedded in the leather to give it a dazzling flavor. Cowboy boots and stockman's whips were on display along with an array of sombreros. Not the fancy, gaudy ones that the tourists usually get for souvenirs, but the working man's hat that a respected "vaquero" would wear. I wish I had more money to get all the things I would

CHAPTER 13

like to have gotten but after a little haggling over the prices, picked out the things I came for and left.

I met Primo a little farther down the street and we decided to get a cold beer before we continued our journey. It was hot, and a little cold refreshment would go a long way, so we popped into a bar called The Blue Fox, just off Revolution Boulevard. It was dark like most bars were, and it took a while for our eyes to adjust. We found a table and sat down while listening to a mariachi band playing on the jukebox in the corner. The place was full of Americans and we fit right in with the crowd. There were a lot of servicemen from San Diego there: marines, sailors in their blues with their front flap button pants, and army G.I.'s, all in uniform. What there wasn't any of were American women, only some Mexican senoritas parading the aisles. We ordered our beers and waited when two girls no older than thirteen sat down and propositioned us. It was a sad sight, and I was sorry we came in for a drink. These girls were so young they didn't even know how to put their makeup on straight. Their lipstick was crooked and flame red. Their rouge was heavy and caked on thick which made them look like clowns from a circus. I was sad, thinking how could this be happening to such little kids and realizing that we were in a different world, and the rules here were not ours. We declined their offer and they straightway hit up some sailors who were of a different frame of mind. We finished our beers and left.

As we were departing TJ, we had to traverse down a steep gorge to the desert below. This mountain road was not for the faint-hearted. The many wooden crosses with flowers planted along the way attested to those who never made it to the bottom, or top, depending on which direction they were going.

We finally reached the bottom and the road straightened, putting us on a direct course for La Rumorosa. The monotony of desert driving is almost hypnotic as the cacti and sagebrush speed by and the heat pelts down from the cloudless sky. In the far distance, I caught sight of a small building with a sign standing in front of it slightly askew from being hit by some drunk or careless driver. The hit caused it to lean precariously close to the building's roof. The paint was peeling off in huge pieces and the weeds were already overrunning the circumference of the building's foundation. It used to be a gas station, but the pumps were long dry and out of service. The hoses were missing and the face plates also gone from most of the three remaining in place.

We parked out front of the station and walked in. I could hear the compressor droning from the top loaded cooler by the counter where I imagined the sodas and beer would be. The pitiful shelves held only the barest of necessities such as canned meat, fish, and beans. Sacks of pinto beans and rice were along the wall and the ever present tequila bottles propped on the counter beside the box that served as a cash register. "Hola," the man inside said as we entered.

"Buenos dias," we replied. We purchased a couple bottles of sodas each and slipped out the door.

We were now leaving La Rumorosa. It was a little drive south to where we were going and with the heat and dust we rode on in silence. The abject poverty I had witnessed as we drove through these little hovels along the road was disheartening, and it only contrasted more the happy nature of the people we encountered.

It was nice to see some giant saguaro cactuses as we hurried down the dirt road we were on; these majestic plants are quickly

CHAPTER 13

disappearing in the United States. Finally, we arrived at the home of the miners and their families. If I thought the town of La Rumorosa was the pits, it was a palace compared to this scene. I could see the main building, or rather a structure, was a teardrop trailer such as the type portrayed in the old black and white Mickey Mouse cartoons. Beside it was several dilapidated cars with missing wheels, doors, and hoods but evidently serving as a shelter for somebody, because there were rags hung over the windows and such for privacy. There were several 55-gallon drums filled with water over to one side swarming with bees and wasps, and one ancient Dodge pick-up their sole source of transportation.

As we pulled up in the clearing out front, several kids of various ages, from barely walking to teenagers, came running to greet us. They were dirty and ragged but with effervescent grins on their faces. Two women appeared from inside the trailer, one obviously pregnant and the other too old for such a condition. They were nervous and said to Primo that their husbands would be here in a few minutes. The men arrived and we all got to greet each other and after some camaraderie they motioned us to follow them.

We walked in the direction they had just come from, and as we walked, one of the men picked up a bag of water and a chrome hub cap off a Volkswagon. He had a small pick stuck in his belt, and we wound our way up a steep slope rising up a few hundred feet from the desert floor. The trail we were on was nothing more than a goat path, and it would be difficult to pass someone traversing the opposite direction.

We reached a spot on the trail where it was leveled off a bit and achieved a small indentation cut into the hillside. It wasn't deep enough to call it a cave or mine, but this is where we stopped. Jorge, the younger of the two, pulled the pick out of his belt and started to dig furiously at a dark vein, about two inches wide, at the back of the inset. He grabbed up the gravelly dirt and dumped it into the hubcap into which he poured some precious water. He swirled the mixture around and around till he shook it violently sideways a couple times exposing some fine specks of color around the edges. His eyes lit up like he had hit the jackpot in Vegas or something, as he showed me his treasure. It would take him ten years of mining like this to fill a thimble full of gold. As an afterthought, he waved his hand and motioned us to follow him once more.

We hiked another thirty feet up the trail to another indentation in the hillside wall. Another display of picking and swirling took place with the same results. Once again he motioned us to walk further up the trail to where he once again began the same ritual. This continued for several sites and it was obvious there was gold there, but it was spread over a large area.

On top of the hill was a vein of garnets six to seven feet wide lying on the ground, and we picked up a bucket full all about the size of children's marbles. Next to the garnets was a white vein of calcium or lime. It was at least twenty feet wide and covered with big chunks of ore, stretching from where we were standing on the crest of the hill and into the valley below. It was a project much larger than I was prepared to handle, even though there was gold there it was from several veins fifteen to twenty feet apart. The chances that they would all meet up in a sizable vein somewhere down the hillside was good. Tons of earth would have to be moved to get there and I didn't have the money to bring up a Caterpillar machine to do it. When we were done for the day, we shared our food and drinks with our new-found friends, and later that evening

CHAPTER 13

hit the road back to civilization.

Sequentially, I talked to some geologists about the whole situation and them said the garnets and lime was a good sign. Gold usually was found close to these minerals and a huge vein could be laying right next to them a few thousand feet into the earth. It may as well have been a few miles into the land as far as I was concerned. I couldn't swing such a massive endeavor. I might have gotten some investors interested in this if it was in the United States, but being in Mexico there was no hope. I was told that if we invested thousands in finding gold, and we actually did find it, there was nothing stopping the Mexican government from moving in and taking everything. It is probably different now, but in those days you never knew.

I knew the miners and their families had high hopes of me investing large amounts of money to get their dream off the ground, but it just wasn't going to happen. The overwhelming odds of it working were more than I was ready to risk. I still remember the time we spent together though, and I hope some investor did come by and make their dreams come true, but it just wasn't to be me.

CHAPTER 14

There were eight of us in the family, all told; my mom and dad, my grandmother on my mom's side, and us five kids. Rod was the eldest at twenty-one then in 1957, Maureen at nineteen, then Rita, seventeen, Dulcie, fifteen, and myself at twelve. Our home at 20 Phyllis Street, buried in a small suburb of Auckland called Mt. Albert, in New Zealand, was small compared to the homes here in California, but we didn't know it. I don't think the square footage of the house was over one thousand feet, but we managed to live well and considered ourselves better off than most. My father was an electrician who owned his own business as an electrical contractor. On the side of our Volkswagen, Combi was written in bold print "H. M. Betham Ltd., Electrical Contractor". The bus wasn't only practical for hauling dad's equipment, but it served as a real bus toting all of us to church each week.

We had an uncle, my dad's little brother Gus, who lived in Redondo Beach, California. He was a real character whom we had never met but knew from all the stories dad used to tell us. He had jumped a steamer at Apia, Samoa, signed up as a roustabout when he was just a teenager, and ended up in California. He managed to build up a gear-cutting shop over the years and now in his fifties, was doing very well. One thing that stood out from all the stories was that Uncle was a hard-living, hard-drinking buckaroo. I didn't really know what a "buckaroo" was, but it sounded exciting. Whenever Gus got a bit drunk, he would find a phone and call Dad, expounding on the beautiful life California offered and how this was the place father needed to be to raise us kids. He went on to tell how this was the land of opportunity and that the sky was the limit when it came to the fortunes that were awaiting us. This went on for years and dad would just go along with it and agree. He would say he would love to, but he was too wrapped up in his business and couldn't just break away no matter how beautiful it sounded.

My parents both were born and raised in Western Samoa, then an English Protectorate. Our heritage goes back hundreds of years there, and even Captain Blye of the ship *Bounty* married a Betham girl named Margaret. My father went to New Zealand for his formal education as an electrician. He was given three choices of a profession by his father, and he was to choose one. The choices were: a doctor, a sea captain, or an electrician. My dad was always queasy at the sight of blood, so that ruled out number one, and just looking at a picture of a ship in rough weather would make him seasick, so there went two, so he became what he was. He always harbored resentment toward his dad because of this lack of choice regarding his own future. Regardless, we were now settled and his profession served us well. I can't picture my dad as anything but what he was, an electrician. One thing I knew about my father was the fact he was impulsive in a lot of ways and this would play out shortly.

The fateful letter that changed our lives arrived on a Friday morning, and my parents read it together. It was from America, Uncle Gus, and the accolades were there full and cumbersome with promises of a land flowing with milk and honey. My parents thought, why not check it out, and decided to go into town and see what the possibilities were. First there was the quota. This was a list of people who wished to immigrate to the United States, and we knew some people who had been waiting for years to be admitted, so the chance of us going was next to nil. None of us

CHAPTER 14

had passports, and the ones my parents had were long expired. We had a business in town consisting of a curio shop which my mom operated to produce supplementary income, and my father's business was repairing appliances. We also had an acre of land we called the orchard since it had a lot of plum trees on it which us kids loved picking in the spring. The house we lived in was a government-owned property that was once a part of some governmental project years before. It was offered to Dad as a freehold property. He signed on, and after years of payments it was ours free and clear. The chances were pretty slim that we would ever see this Promised Land.

The man told dad that since he was a Samoan National he would shoot to the top of the list regarding the quota. If we drove to Wellington, a city at the farthest southern tip of the North Island, we could get our passports in a day or two. This entailed getting immunization shots, having pictures taken, and completing reams of paperwork, not including the trip down to the airport which was no small task in those days. He also mentioned as an afterthought that there just happened to be eight empty seats on the flight out of Auckland on the following Tuesday. Did I mention my dad was impulsive? He didn't hesitate. "I'll take them," he answered. My mom, who always had something to say about almost everything, was struck dumb at that instant and it wasn't until they were halfway home that she burst out crying. It had finally sunk in, while Dad was merrily driving along, as pleased as punch with his splendid decision, and didn't have a clue why she was so upset. Mom was always the practical one in their relationship and Dad the dreamer.

They reached home that evening, Mom's eyes still red from crying, and Dad called us all together and proudly announced we were all going to America on Tuesday. We didn't believe him but then seeing Mom's countenance, we knew something was up.

The task ahead was monumental to say the least and, unfortunately, the brunt of it fell on Mom. We had to sell everything we owned and reduce all our possessions down to two suitcases each. This meant selling the house, orchard business, curio shop/office, furniture, piano, utilities, pots and pans, china sets, silverware and the list goes on, in four days.

My parents, being God-fearing church members, put the matter before God. I'm sure Dad took some heat for asking such an outrageous request of Him, but Dad was very familiar with the phrase, "With God, all things are possible". I know one thing for sure: God kept Mom from losing her mind in those hectic days of packing. She started to break down after feverishly getting things packed. We had relatives over, and the things we didn't sell she gave away. We didn't have yard sales then, so everything was done by word of mouth.

The only media we had in those days were the radio and newspapers, and the radio was rife with catchy commercials advertising this or that product. One such ad was for Coleman's mustard which ended with a little jingle stating, "Coleman's got the mustard." Mom got the phrase, "Coleman's got the mustard" stuck in her head, and she kept saying it over and over. She was a Buddhist monk repeating his monotonous mumblings to an unseen deity. She couldn't help it, she was traumatized, and nothing relieved her symptoms till we finally disembarked for America.

As unbelievable as it was, we got everything sold and otherwise disencumbered, except for Dad's business. He had a buyer that wanted him to stay on board to help him through the first few

CHAPTER 14

months to acclimate him to this new company. Dad said that was impossible, but he did stay back for a few days to help, and he caught up with us later in Samoa.

The day arrived and we headed for the airport. We were traveling on Pan American and the plane was waiting on the tarmac with the stairs leading up to the front door. We had some relatives that came to see us off at the airport. Of course, we were decked out with the leis up to our noses, which to remove would have been an insult, so they were endured until we finally climbed on board. Traveling in those days was not like today. The plane, a four-engine propeller job, I think it was called a Constellation, was not full of amenities such as are available today, but the stewardess did give me a set of gold wings to pin on as we entered, and I thought that was pretty neat. I must have looked a sight because I had on three shirts, two pairs of pants, and a sweater. Mom didn't have enough room in my suitcases to fit with all my stuff, so being the practical person she was, she had me wear it so we wouldn't have to leave it behind. I looked like the Michelin Tire guy or Frosty the snowman so puffed up my arms wouldn't hang down by my sides; they kind of stuck out a bit. This was okay in New Zealand, but we were headed for the tropics, and I would probably sweat to death dressed like this.

We were served a TV dinner on board and this was my first encounter with fast food packaging. My eyes were transfixed on the far engine of the plane, watching black oil flowing from the engine housing forming a steady stream about six inches wide. I knew I was just a kid, but common sense tells you this wasn't normal, and how come the other engine wasn't leaking? I was assured that this was not uncommon and not to worry. The flight took many hours and I was beginning to think we would never see land. The jets we have now fly the same trip in less than half the time.

Our first stop was Nadi, Fiji. A direct flight was not an option, so we stayed there with some of my mother's family until we could catch the flying boat to Apia, Samoa a few days later. I remember playing hide and seek with my new-found cousins and while dashing around in the dark of the evening, I could feel these spongy things under my feet squishing as I ran around the yard. I didn't know what I was stepping on until I reached the front porch, and in the light I saw thousands of frogs all over the grass. These were cane frogs that were brought in to eradicate some pest but instead became a bigger pest themselves. I will never forget the impression it left on me seeing those frogs carpeting the yard there in Fiji.

The flying boat was nothing more than an old army PBY that was converted over for commercial passenger use by some entrepreneur. We sat in our seats and looked out a porthole on the side. As we began to taxi out to the open sea, the water swooshed over the porthole and I felt as though I was in a submarine going down, instead of a plane going up. The trip was uneventful and we touched down in the bay right outside of Apia. The plane taxied to the dock where we disembarked.

We were met by my dad's parents and a slew of "aiga", or relatives, wanting to see us, especially Mom and Granny who were born and raised in the islands. We all migrated to Lotopa, my dad's village and homestead where more people awaited us, with a huge array of food and drinks all set up for us on tables. The food was different, even though Mom managed to introduce us to most of it during our childhood. There was the taro and cooked bananas, fish

CHAPTER 14

and meat and a dish called "palusami" made from cooked taro leaves with coconut milk and onions. This was cholesterol heaven, and being just a kid, I didn't care. In those days we didn't worry about things like fat and arterial sclerosis, things we had no idea existed. People just naturally keeled over from heart attacks and Samoans were pretty much poster children on top of the list.

In time, we did suffer from our lavish diet and my sisters, Maureen and Rita, and I all got huge boils on our legs and backs which were painful and unsightly. Mom just put hot bread poultices on them and overnight it sucked out the core and all the infection. One I had on my leg was left with a red hole in my thigh as clean as a whistle. Mom's home remedies amazed me at times and this was one of those times.

Our stay in Samoa was blissful and relaxing. Meeting so many relatives and friends and the endless parties and get togethers were surreal. When Dad showed up, it began all over again. My mother's brother lived in Apia and his son was about my age. His name was Michael and we became fast friends even though we were cousins. We earned a couple of nicknames and neither one was complimentary. I think mine was "Hellion" or something close. I would pick up Samoan words from the grownups and ask Mom or Dad what they meant. For some reason, we kids were never taught the language and we all suffered from this. All our cousins could rattle off Samoan as their second language, but us "palagis" or white folk didn't have a clue as to what they were saying. We became the brunt of more than a few jokes and none of us liked it much.

My granny was born in Samoa when it was under the German rule and she had to learn German in school. Now there is low German and high German, which I didn't know existed, and she was taught the high German in school, which many marveled at whenever she spoke it. She was a wonderful woman and her life spanned such a vast period of increased knowledge. She was born in 1885 when the sailing ships were the only mode of international travel. They had a buggy and two horses to pull it from Lufilufi, her village, to Apia, the capital city. She endured several wars and the plague where half the population of the island died. She remembers as a child being taken on a German man-of-war for protection and having to sleep under the huge guns on deck during the battle with the British over sovereignty of the island. She remembered the hardened sailors chuckling over her and her friend, kneeling down and saying their prayers under these huge guns before retiring for the night. Her life spanned the horse and buggy age to seeing Neil Armstrong on TV land on the moon in 1962, shortly before her death. She spoke English and German and Samoan fluently and could read and write them too. She preferred her German Bible over the others, I think because it spoke to her in a more matter-of-fact way. I think of her with fond thoughts and wonder at the gracious life she lived.

The final leg of our journey quickly came, and we once again boarded the plane for Hawaii, our port of entry into the United States. Hawaii wasn't a state yet, but it was a United States Territory, and Honolulu acted as an entering point to our final destination. I received a document stating that we had crossed the International Date Line, and it was pretty enough for a frame and to be hung on the wall. It was a nice perk from Pan Am. and I still have it. As I said, traveling was a big deal in 1957, and it's a shame some of the niceties are now gone.

CHAPTER 14

After Hawaii, we made one last stop in the middle of nowhere called Canton Island. It was just big enough to be a gas station for flights between Hawaii and California. We arrived in Los Angeles in the month of June 1957, and Uncle Gus and some of our parents other friends were there to meet us. We gathered up our suitcases and loaded them into the "Scorpion Jet", Uncle's 1952 Ford Woody. He took us to his home on Ruhland Avenue in Redondo Beach, where we met his family and I saw television for the first time. It was Saturday morning and Mighty Mouse was in full swing. I was disappointed my cowboy heroes weren't at the airport to greet me, and the western towns with their saloons and livery stables were absent also, but I would meet them later at Knott's Berry Farm. That was when it was free and the berry farm was still producing berries. It was America and we had made it.

The whole trip was fantastic and the life we found here wasn't too far from the truth that Uncle Gus kept telling us. This really is the land of milk and honey, the promised land.

CHAPTER 15

One thing that stands out in my mind regarding my childhood was the family worship time my parents insisted we children attend. It was mandatory and no matter how hard I tried to ditch worship, my parents had a solution to rectify the situation and get me back on track. The time spent was usually just after sundown or after supper depending on what season it was. During the winter months, sunset came pretty early so we had worship before supper and vice versa. Sometimes Mom would read us some story from a religious book. The younger ones, mainly my sister Dulcie and myself, would ask her to read a chapter out of "Uncle Arthur's Bedtime Stories". After the reading, Dad would always end the worship time with a prayer. He always included each individual kid in his prayer and I think I got a lot of overtime during these monologues due to my restless nature. I didn't really believe God was that interested in what I was doing, but future events over the years have convinced me otherwise. Our family is living proof that "a family that prays together stays together."

We had only been in our new homeland a few years and already my older brother, Rod, had joined the navy and had done two tours to Japan. He had married a beautiful girl from our church and settled down a few blocks from the family home. My sister, Rita, was introduced to one of Rod's navy buddies, Ted Hardy, a farm boy from Nebraska. It wasn't too long after that they were married and had gone back to the corn husker's state to begin their own family. Rita was the first to get married and soon they had three girls and two boys. Their farm house was less than spitting distance from the main railhead that ran through their section of the country. The three o'clock high-baller train that rumbled through each morning, we felt, must have contributed to their large family.

It was the middle of winter and all of us were sitting around the kitchen table. We had just finished a large meal and as usual the talk usually carried on for an hour or two depending on the subject matter. Out of the blue dad came up with this great idea, "Let's drive to Nebraska and visit Rita and Ted." We had recently purchased a brand new 1959 Pontiac Star Chief and I think Dad wanted a chance to check it out. Rita was ready to have her first born child so mom was agreeable to the plan.

Mom loved this car and was instrumental in choosing the salmon pink color with the same interior. I think the color was designated as "Desert Rose" by General Motors, but that didn't matter to Mom as much as the silver threads in the carpet and seat covers. It was a beauty and it had all the power we ever needed. I remember the day we brought it home from the dealers and we all got a chance to drive it. My cousin, Theresa, was visiting and wanted to drive it also so once again we piled in as she took the wheel. She had a reputation for running red lights and the fact that she had never hit anyone or was never hit by anyone else was a miracle in itself. We made sure she stopped at the light and everyone breathed a breath of air until the light turned green. She shoved the throttle to the floor and after a second or two turned to me and said, "There's something wrong with the car, it won't go." White smoke was billowing from the rear of the car as the tires spun uncontrollably. I yelled at her to let up on the gas or she was going to kill us. When she did the car shot forward as if at the drag

CHAPTER 15

strip and we hurtled down Prairie Avenue past the Golf Course and into Hawthorne, the neighboring city.

To say we were the prime examples of the ones that had just fallen off the turnip truck would have been an understatement. Naive was a nice way of stating the obvious. I had my driver's license and Dad usually let me do the driving so he could enjoy the scenery. We packed some clothes and grabbed a map and put some food in a bag, piled into the car and headed off to Nebraska. There was Mom and Dad and myself in the front seat and Granny and Dulcie and Maureen in the back. After reviewing the map, I asked Dad what route he wanted me to take. I said we could go the southern route on the 10-East or the northern route on the 40-East, or we could go through some real beautiful landscapes even a little further north than that. Mom said let's see the lovely mountains and trees so the northern route it was.

Global warming hadn't taken effect yet as far as I could tell. It was early 1959 and the winters in the Rockies were still pretty severe. We were as happy as clams and none of us had ever seen snow before. We figured why not now? We were from one of the countries known for its cold weather, but the area on the North Island where we were from was where it didn't snow. It got cold enough to chill you to the bone, and frost lay on the ground an inch thick, but it didn't snow. I rechecked the map and it said there was a pass called, "Bridal Veil Pass", where we could cut through and still get to Nebraska en-route. The route was all set and we were heading off like lambs to the slaughter without a care in the world. I've heard it said God has a special place in His heart for the innocent, and we, all combined, were claiming an acre or two.

The trip was turning out to be really special and our spirits were high as we talked about various subjects from Rita's impending delivery to what snow must feel like. Little did we realize how soon both topics would be answered. The further north we traveled the cooler it got. I had been using the car's heater for quite a few miles and every hundred miles or so I would crank it up a notch. We reached the base of the Rockies and started our ascent, but not before we all piled out at the first sign of snow and tromped around in it a bit to get the full effect. With our ruddy cheeks and freezing fingers, we re-entered the Pontiac and scooted down the road. "Turn the heater up," someone said, and I did once more.

The higher we got, the less traffic we encountered, and we thought, "Gee, we practically have the whole road to ourselves." As we attained more altitude, it began to snow. The shrieks in the car were deafening and the excitement contagious as we barreled along, almost alone now, on the white carpet ahead. I began to get a little unnerved as the yellow line in the road slowly disappeared and was replaced with the white "Manna from Heaven". I had the heater going full blast and didn't really feel the effect as much as before. We were now the only people on the highway and it was snowing in earnest.

The truckers who I crossed paths with periodically gave me some comfort but now they were gone and we were alone. We had never heard of snow chains and blizzard warnings and all the other things associated with mountain weather. It wasn't until the windshield wipers couldn't clear the snow from the window that it began to sink in we might be in a tad bit of trouble. Just then the dash went ding and the green "cold light" came on, showing me that the engine was cold and not to rev it up until the light went out. This was intended to keep the driver from flooring it until the

CHAPTER 15

engine was warmed up each morning, not dinging in the middle of a drive across country. I thought it handy that there were some poles along the highway that helped me center the car on the road and away from the burms. I found out later they were there for the snow plows to keep a reference to the curbs, not me.

It got quiet in the cab and all talk of this and that ceased. We hadn't seen another soul in miles and the snow was about a foot deep. We were still plowing along at fifty to sixty miles an hour not daring to stop in the event we would never get going again. The fact that the snowflakes were so huge or the visibility so limited wasn't germane to the problem at hand and that was, of course, our survival.

It was time to pull out the big guns and that's just what we did. Dad said, "Let's pray." There is a degree of comfort derived from handing the reigns to someone else to do the steering. Even though I was still driving, I felt second in command that day as we flew down the highway during one of the biggest blizzards in recent history on that pass.

This kept up for many more miles and the snow never got deeper and the falling snow never heavier. It was as if we were in limbo until we started our descent. The snow finally thinned out and the drifts came less often. Finally, we reached the base of the mountains and the green light went out. Dad always taught us that if we asked God for something, we should always thank Him for His answer no matter the outcome. We stopped the car and thanked Him for His guidance and deliverance that day in the Rockies.

With the Rockies behind us we were headed for the flatlands of Nebraska. The roads were alright but not like they are today and we had a lot of construction going on in most states. I think there was a big push to improve the highway system throughout all the forty-nine states. This was 1959 and Alaska was just admitted to the union in August. Hawaii would also be added to the states soon, and during post-war reconstruction, I believe infrastructure, highways, were at the top of the list. The problem was that there were not a lot of private businesses keeping up with them and gas stations were few and far between in some areas. We happened to be in one of those areas. It was nightfall and we had just entered Nebraska. We had filled up the gas tank at the base of the Rockies and now we were in Nebraska and we were running short of gas and had a long way to go yet. I told everyone to keep their eyes peeled for a gas station 'cause we were running low. Many were sighted, but they were closed for the night. The landscape was bleak and monotonous with a farmhouse and silo popping up every once in a while but no gas stations. This kept on for miles and the gas gauge was dead empty. I said, "Dad, we need gas and I sure don't want to run out right here in the middle of nowhere."

"Time for the big guns again," Dad said. "It's me again, Lord, and we sure could use your help once again."

I drove on as if an egg was between my foot and the gas pedal, trying to utilize every trick I knew to conserve gas as we drove on. It was over 300 miles we traveled that way, on empty, and passing closed gas stations mile after mile. I got Toyota Prius mileage out of high performance 389 cubic inch Pontiac Star Chief four door tank, fully loaded with people and luggage. This was another miracle granted through God's grace and His tender mercies. I mentioned the fact we claimed a huge chunk of God's heart and He never let us down. These memories will be forever implanted in my mind and I will share them as often as I can.

CHAPTER 15

The car full of vagabonds finally reached their destination and we piled out in front of Rita and Teds place in Endicott, tired but happy. We had traversed a large section of the United States and had seen a lot of new things. We were wiser and in the future we would take into account the season and weather conditions before we would head out blindly like we had this time. I think it goes back to those worship episodes I tried to ditch as a youth. I felt they were unnecessary and boring but as I grew I began to see the wisdom of two parents dedicated to raising their kids in a way pleasing to God.

CHAPTER 16

Uncle Gus was a colorful character to say the least and his antics were always a source of entertainment for the whole family. The party never really got started until Gus showed up with his Martin guitar and a bottle of hooch. He dabbled in real estate and bought several hundred acres out in Lancaster California because someone told him they were going to build the new international airport there and land values would skyrocket. He drove out once in a while to check on it and to show us the future airport location. His favorite mode of transport to this site was his 1952 Ford Wagon that he dubbed "The Scorpion Jet". The Jet was a wooden-sided station wagon that the surfers around his home in Redondo Beach liked to call a "Woody". His home he referred to as "Gopher Acres." The choice was obvious.

We had settled into our new home, a new tract house in North Torrance and were laying some cement in our backyard. My dad had the bright idea to pour the cement into the shape of a giant shield. His father had done some research over the years and had produced the family crest. He had gone back as far as the year 639 with Egbert, or some such monarch as our royal ancestor and Dad figured why not pour the slab to commemorate it. One corner of the yard looked a little bare so he said he wanted to think about it a while but wanted something special there. We couldn't pour the whole back yard in one shot so divided it up into six-foot square segments, separated with redwood two by fours. Dad got hold of some colored cement and capped the tops of each square with red, blue, green and yellow. The men from our church all pitched in to help and Mom made a super dinner for all after the job was done. One "brother" was a little needy and a few weeks back Dad thought he would help him out by giving him a nice suit to wear to church. The fellow showed up that day to pour cement while dressed in the suit Dad had given him. He did the work dressed to the nines. We had a colorful yard for many years until time faded it out, one square at a time, all to cement gray.

It was a few weeks later that Dad came home with a giant cast iron tub he maneuvered around to the "bare corner" with my help. We dug a large hole to fit the container into and sunk it down into the lip after Dad had laid some pipes and EMT for some wiring. We lugged in sheets of Palos Verdes rock and boulders. After some weeks of fitting and masonry and a lot of ingenuity, he had finally finished. He called out to Mom to come see. Then he flipped the switch and we watched as a beautiful waterfall cascaded down the rock face and dumped into the tub which was covered around the edges with ferns and grasses. It was beautiful and my admiration of my dad's abilities grew. He was good and he was fast and seldom had to do a job over, if at all.

He had a job once with a contractor who was a real taskmaster. Time was money and Dad never disappointed him. The other men didn't appreciate his work ethic because it made them look bad. Dad would wire a complete house by himself while it took them the same time, combined, to do the same. I remember once when Frank, my brother-in-law, was working with us on a project. He had to space something one foot apart and was looking for a measuring tape to mark the distance. Dad was passing by and said, "Give me the pencil", and with two strokes marked out the spot and said, "That's close enough." Frank, not to be put off, got the tape

CHAPTER 16

and measured between the strokes and it was smack on. Not one sixteenth off. That's my dad.

We were nailing studs one time and Dad as usual was giving it a one hundred and ten percent effort. He was distracted for a moment and smacked his thumb with his hammer so hard it spat blood in a semicircle around it and his fingernail was hanging on by a thread of skin. After the perfunctory, "Hell's Bells", he pulled the nail off, threw it away and took some electrical tape which he wound around his thumb to stop the bleeding. The operation took five minutes and he was back in full swing. Today, for most men, it would require a two-week medical leave and workman's compensation benefits.

We knew that Disneyland had just opened a few years before but the cost to go there was out of our reach. Even though it was only an hour drive from our home, this was before the 10 freeway was built, so it might as well have been in Timbuktu, Egypt. There was, however, another place we could visit for free not too far from Disneyland, called Knott's Berry Farm. Uncle Gus had told us that this farmer had brought a complete ghost town from the desert and transported it to his farm in Anaheim. There was a restaurant there that fixed the most delicious chicken and we ought to go and see it.

In New Zealand whenever we visited anyplace, whether the zoo or movie theater, Dad always dressed up in his suit. It showed the respect, he said, so we didn't argue; we just humored him, and accepted his beliefs and carried on. He had a black fedora hat he wore as part of his outfit along with vest and pocket watch and lace up-brougham shoes. This particular suit was navy blue with pinstripes and all he needed was spats and a submachine gun to finish off the illusion of Clyde Barrow.

The Berry Farm those days consisted of the restaurant, Ghost Town, a berry stand and some curio shops where you could purchase a souvenir or two. There was a blacksmith shop where you could buy a horseshoe ring or horseshoe puzzle all made there on the premises. There weren't the rides and other entertainments, like the stagecoach and steam train; that all came much later. We all split up to seek out the things that interested each one of us. We would meet back at the restaurant later that day and have lunch together. The appointed time came and we couldn't find Dad. We searched for him together and found a crowd of people in front of the saloon apparently interested in some particular feature. I pushed my way up front and was awestruck by what I saw. Dad was posing with people who thought he was part of the Berry Farm. Dad, always willing to oblige, was smiling away and posing with groups of women and children all anxious to be photographed with the gangster he must be portraying. The whole afternoon was a kick for Dad and if Walter Knott had seen the interest that he was creating out in front of his saloon, he would have hired Dad on the spot. I have a picture of Dad at the zoo back in New Zealand, with us kids, and I swear he was the spitting image of John Wayne himself.

One attribute Dad had that was a constant annoyance for mom was his colorful use of the King's English if ever he whacked himself or wanted to emphasize a point. I can still envision her reprimanding him for one outburst or another and Dad looking sheepish with a big grin on his face. He wasn't going to change and we all knew it, for he came by this habit through the rite of passage. Grandpa was worse than Dad. He was raised in Samoa, the same as Granny, and went to the same German school as she did. He learned more German than she because he could cuss

CHAPTER 16

in both English and German, a fault she willfully omitted from her vocabulary. He preferred the German, I think, because it was somehow more descriptive.

Camp time for our local church conference arrived each year usually in the middle of summer when the weather was the warmest. The excitement it aroused was always uplifting and inspiring. The campground, located twenty to thirty miles from town, was situated next to a river and donated by a farmer who enjoyed the revelry this event produced. There were high-powered ministers that were brought in for this event, and the music always was loud and excellent and the best part of camp meetings as far as I was concerned. The conference planners always asked Dad if he would do the electrical wiring for the main tent and the rows of individual tents each family rented for the week long hiatus. Even though I was only a little guy, still in elementary school, I was a big help for Dad as his "gopher" to fetch tools or equipment. Dad would procure a large generator, usually some old World War II surplus model that produced the electricity and distributed the power from this main supply.

It was during the height of the meetings when things started to go amok. The generator failed, and the power was gone. This meant the PA system was down and with no loudspeaker, there was no meeting. This was a real emergency and dad was plumb in the middle of it. Now, Dad was a cracker-jack electrician but just a mediocre mechanic. The engine running the generator wouldn't run, and he was furiously trying to rectify the problem. Unbeknown to Dad, the ministers thought it prudent to all gather together and had a special prayer to seek the Lord's help in restoring the power. They all congregated outside the main tent and formed a circle a stone's throw from the generator. Dad, still fighting the mechanical monster, was getting more frustrated, and shorter tempered as he lay on the ground under the misbehaving piece of equipment. Just as the men of God were starting their supplications, Dad's patience ran out, and he couldn't control himself any longer. He let fly a slew of rhetoric that would make a hardened criminal blush. He never used the downright crass words we were all taught not to even think. He had a repertoire of sayings from, "Hell's Bells and Buggy Wheels", his favorite, to "Son of a …", and more.

He realized too late that he wasn't alone, and the audience couldn't have been worse. I never saw my dad turn so many shades of red in such a short time. The ministers, I'm sure suppressing a laugh, stopped their praying and one old soul quietly said, "We'll put in a good word for you too, brother Hector." The power was shortly restored and I know for a fact this wasn't the last time God used a humble electrician to fulfill a need when a serious problem arose. Dad's antics subsided for a time from this experience but were never entirely eradicated.

CHAPTER 17

My Aunt Maud had a passel of kids ranging from Theresa, the eldest, to Jacques, the baby, with Earnest, Joe, Paul, Richard, Eva and Hector in the middle. Richard was the closest to me in age, and we got into a lot of mischief together. He was affectionately referred to as Pua'a or in English, the pig. He did have a ravenous appetite and weighed in at around 350 pounds. He got a job with the Merchant Marines as (what else?) a cook. His travels took him all over the world but mostly he had to stay on board as leave was seldom given to the kitchen help. He had a pretty good salary and with no place to spend it, he arrived back home with a sizable chunk of change.

Working on old cars was our passion and the one we were tricking out was Paul's '56 Ford custom. It was a two-door coupe with a 312 cubic inch V-8 engine and "three on the tree", or column shift transmission. It was in primer grey and sported a set of mag wheels. Paul enlisted my help in jazzing it up because I was considered the hot rod guru and came cheap. Paul had a reasonably good job, and what he didn't drink away he stashed away for the big renovation of his car. If cars were his hobby, drinking was his passion. Seldom a weekend went by that a keg or two of beer wasn't consumed at his apartment overlooking the main drag in El Porto, a small beach community next to Redondo Beach, California. There were the regulars who always came and never paid, and passers-on-through who were always welcome and seldom came with any booze of their own, either. Paul almost footed the bill for the whole crowd, and I feel it stems from his Samoan background of one-for-all and all-for-one. The Musketeers, I firmly believe, got their ethics from the Samoans, only in Paul's case it was mostly "one for all", seldom "all for one". One memory I still have of these riotous gatherings is the squishing of my footsteps as I picked my way around the sleeping drunks and empty cans of beer, on the soaked carpet flooring the following morning.

We always did our automotive work at "Momsies" place, Auntie Maud's driveway. It was the only place big enough to work and because she would always have something good to eat, hot and ready, when we were done for the day. She had the kind of voice that carried for miles and if you were too close when she had something to say, you had better cover the ear closest to her. She had some pretty tough times in her life and I can only marvel at how she coped with so many kids and very little help from her husband. Uncle Dick always had a jug of wine next to him, and I mean always.

Uncle Dick was pretty mellow and never really got mad unless the little ones started scrapping at his feet over some toy or piece of candy. He would dutifully pick each one up by the scruff of the neck and drop kick them through the front door and into the front yard. Grandpa, the father of Momsie and Dad, lived with Momsie and usually stayed in his recliner in the middle of the front room. The little ones knew not to get too close to grandpa. Depending on what mood he happened to be in, a good cuff on the back of the head is what you got for straying too close to his chair. If you had the audacity to say, "What was that for?" He would retort, "Come back again and I'll give you another." All in all, it was a functioning society with a lot of love to offset the occasional wallop on the head, given for whatever reason.

CHAPTER 17

Paul had saved up a couple of thousand dollars and we were ready to begin our overhaul. We picked the best cam and lifters for the job plus pistons and crank, and most importantly, the intake manifold. We wanted a tri-power set up with three carburetors instead of one. This single feature was the coolest looking as well as being the single most productive item for increased horsepower except a NOs system, or Nitrous Oxide. Getting the parts was half the fun and as we hunted through catalogue after catalogue for the best prices and product we were finally ready to begin.

We pulled the engine out and started stripping it down to the essential pieces so we could then start building it back up again with all the new goodies installed. This operation wasn't without its drawbacks, such as the oily mess incurred all over Momsie's driveway. Now, Momsie was a devout Catholic and attended Mass as often as she could, but this situation was pushing her piousness to new limits. She was, after all, a product of Grandpa, and we knew exactly what waters we were sinking into quickly. " We'll clean it up right away," we all pleaded, but the horror of the driveway was more than all the pleading in the world could atone for. We had to just shut up and take the lecture she was now dishing out at volume 110 on the Richter scale. I'm sure the neighbors two miles down the road heard every word loud and clear. After she had run out of the dialogue, she started to ratchet it down a notch or two. All she had left was some reiterations on the important items and finally just a, "You had better watch out in the future. Now get it cleaned up and come in for dinner, I have some fried chicken and mashed potatoes and gravy for you." That was Momsie; loud and harsh as nails, but a heart of gold underneath.

We put in a lot of weekends on that old Ford, and the day

arrived when we were ready for it to fire up. The battery was flat from sitting so long so we borrowed one out of the closest car available. I had some gas in a juice can ready to prime the center carburetor. Paul cranked it over and I trickled some gas in as the engine backfired and blew a flame two feet in the air taking my eyebrows and some of my head-of-hair with it. I shot back, and faithful to my family tradition let loose with a stream of blue verbage fitting for the occasion. The pop from the backfire brought Momsie to the back door, and after listening to my off-color oration she let the neighbors know what she thought of this kind of talk. If I had been a Catholic, I'm sure she would have made me make penitence there and then. We re-timed the distributor and it fired up for the first time and it ran fine. Paul revved it up a few times and kept it moving at a fast rate to break the cam in. I stood back with my new hairdo and missing eyebrows and grinned from ear to ear.

Now that the car was running the brothers and sisters, and all the kids from the neighborhood, wanted to climb in for the maiden voyage. Grandpa managed to hobble out to the stoop and Momsie too watched as we launched out of the driveway for the first time in weeks. You could hear Momsie yelling after us to, "Take it easy and don't get in trouble with the cops," for at least two blocks which was no small feat since we hadn't installed the mufflers yet.

Paul stuck to the back streets and after a few passes up and down the block, wanted to see how it ran when he opened up the two other carbs, as yet not engaged. The old Ford literally jumped forward as the "whooooop" of the carburetors howled when they all kicked in at once. The whooping from the back seat also added to the cacophony already sounding out in the front. We must have

CHAPTER 17

been doing seventy-five miles an hour down the side street when without warning "POW", the tranny blew, and we coasted to a stop alongside the curb. Paul didn't care, he was still jacked up from the hellacious performance we had just endured. Everyone piled out and we pushed the car the mile and a half to home. We were glad we let them come along for the ride because now they could earn their keep by pushing iron. We limped home and back into the driveway which was now becoming a familiar crib for the '56.

We purchased several more Ford trannys from wrecking yards and we kept blowing second gear which was a weak point ever since they were made from the factory. The four-speed was just released in the new Mustangs and were way too expensive for Paul, even if he quit drinking for a year or two; well, maybe a year, anyway.

Richard had arrived home from a tour overseas and was loaded. The first thing he did was buy a brand new Mustang Coupe. It was a beauty, painted canary yellow with black interior. He paid a huge down payment because his credit rating was far from acceptable but with a hefty down the dealer relented and gave him the car. It was a 389 cubic inch engine with a four-barrel carburetor and four on the floor. It had bucket seats and a console between them with a neat silver roll up thingy where you kept gloves or cigarettes, or in Pua'a's case, a joint or two. We would cruise that car all over southern California, from Hollywood on the weekend nights to the beaches and parks in the daytime. We would race anything that pulled up next to us with an inkling to do so. We seldom lost.

We were so used to driving junkers, this new-car thing was hard to get used to and harder yet to forget when the dream ended, which was to be only too soon in Pua'a's case. Monthly payments were not a thing he was accustomed to and harder yet to accomplish.

It was after several months of this that he became depressed and wanted out. He conspired with Paul and between the two of them he reluctantly parked the Mustang in a deserted field and set fire to it. Pua'a was not only delinquent in his car payments but his insurance payments as well. His plan almost backfired on him, no pun intended, but finally the insurance company paid it off and he was again debt free. Not a scenario I was happy with and that is why I was left out of the picture when this plan was instigated.

Paul miraculously came up with a new Mustang tranny for his '56 Coupe, which we quickly installed. The difference it made was short of awesome, and we soon were racing all comers. If Richard still had the Mustang, he wouldn't be able to beat the '56 hands down. We knew that scene would never play out. It wasn't long before we started blowing drive lines and then rear ends. These problems we faced each time they surfaced. There was no way to build the car like we should have from the beginning, doing all the drive train at once. We were happy with this because we got to drive it each time until it required more attention further down the road. It also gave Paul time to build up his bankroll until it was needed later in time.

Paul kept his prized '56 for many years and we all treasured the fun times we spent in the shotgun seat or behind the wheel. He did rack up a pile of speeding tickets, but he didn't care, his car was his best friend in many ways and he always referred to it as his baby, a fact borne out over the years.

CHAPTER 18

William Jamerson was known by most of the islanders as Willie. His talents were numerous, and he could do anything from shipbuilding to construction. He, like so many other talented men, had some vices that minimized his accomplishments. He met my grandmother, Anna, while she tended her store in the village of Lufilufi thirty miles east of Apia, the capital city, and the largest port of Samoa. Thirty miles isn't such a distance these days, but then it was a half-day journey on horseback over a dirt road seldom maintained by the government. It wasn't with any ill will when referring to her village as being out in the sticks. It was just an accepted fact.

My granny, who was very young during this time, was exceptionally beautiful. My mother would hear tales of how pretty she was as a young girl, but then the old women would add, " But her mother, Mary, she was a real beauty." The village was so proud her as if they had invested some time and energy in her creation. Her dad was a German sea captain named Billingberg and her mother, Mary Marshall, the daughter of a prestigious chief, Poloai. Billingberg wanted to marry Mary and said he was heading back to Germany to deliver his ship and he would be back as soon as possible so they could wed. This was during the first world war and times were dangerous.

Word was sent back to Samoa that his ship was sunk, and he did not survive. He never knew his sweetheart was pregnant when he sailed, and I feel to this day his kinfolk would have loved to find out he was survived by a daughter even if she were illegitimate. Since her parents were never married, it caused my grandmother a lot of shame and to her dying day she seldom talked of it. She remembers as a child walking to school with a friend, the postmaster called out to her, and thinking he was doing her a good deed, handed her a picture of her father. She remembers looking at a portrait of a man in uniform, and being overcome with shame and anger, tore it up in pieces and stomped on them, a decision she bitterly regretted.

Jamerson was smitten with Anna and spent a lot of time visiting the little store there in Lufilufi. He had discovered a precious pearl hid away in the backcountry and he was set on having her for his own some day. The problem was that he was already married, and my grandmother would have nothing to do with him unless he divorced his wife first. He said he wasn't happy, and his wife was on another island and he hadn't seen her in years. Nevertheless, Anna was firm and refused all his advances with aplomb determination. Willie figured he would endear himself to Anna. With his many talents and offered to build her a schooner so she could sail back and forth to Apia, and anywhere else in the Pacific Rim, in fact if she desired.

Copra was an export widely grown and harvested on the island, and Anna was shipping tons of it herself on a regular basis to supplement her profits at the store. She was a frugal businesswoman and had stashed away several thousand "marks", the currency used at the time. She agreed, but only on one condition, and that was that she would pay for all the materials and time invested in its construction. Willie figured that being nearby with Anna, she would relent, and he would be able to woo her and hopefully win her or seduce her somehow. Anna's own beginning was enough to keep her staunch in her refusals and unbeknown to Willie his advances were an exercise in futility.

CHAPTER 18

The schooner was a magnificent piece of work and over the months it took him to build it, he added several innovations he designed himself. The one I specifically remember Granny telling me about was a retracting keel that was used when approaching the reef, which surrounded most islands. You could crank the keel up into the body of the boat and glide over the reef without hanging up and floundering as so many other ships did. The schooner quickly paid for itself and Jamerson was no closer to his goal than before he started.

His next scheme was to build Anna an enormous house with her store occupying the bottom floor. He proposed the idea and again Anna said only on one condition. He readily agreed and began construction. Anna paid for the lumber and hardware and all the expenses as they occurred. This relationship with Willie lasted for seven years and his determination was measured solely by his love or lust of this beautiful country girl.

The house was finished and it was beautiful, a two-storied structure with a veranda surrounding the whole upper floor. The view of the ocean, a stone's throw from the veranda, was magnificent as well as the river flowing into the ocean a few hundred feet from the east side of the house. The river was used for bathing as well as washing and provided a sanctuary from the heat and humidity during the monsoon season.

I never knew why Jamerson didn't divorce his wife, but it must have been frustrating for him because he was constantly being denied any serious advances towards Anna. After seven years I think my grandmother was fed up with the constant excuses and unfounded reasons for his marital status. His frustrations were fed by his continued drinking which only got worse as the situation became more hopeless. Anna finally told him not to come around anymore until he squared away his encumbrances and was free to marry.

I guess sea captains and officers had a penchant for this little village since so many children were their offspring either by marriage or, too often, the result of a "fiafia", or village celebration, of some kind.

There was word in Apia about this ravishing beauty living in the backwoods somewhere east of the city. It was a typical subject for the local businessmen who gathered at the local bar for a cold one. There must have been some truth to the rumor because a German officer overheard these remarks and decided to investigate them for himself. His name was Fritz von Reiche and he was from a wealthy family situated east of Berlin.

He procured a horse and set out to find this anomaly tucked away in the back country of Samoa, a decision he never regretted. It says in the Bible that a man found a treasure in his neighbor's field and he went and sold all he had to buy the field and the treasure for himself. This was a lesson from the Master and it was to relate to the heavenly kingdom and its value to us mortals. Well, Fritz found his treasure and he was willing to give everything he had to get it. Heaven is in the eyes of the beholder and his eyes beheld a sight that left him awestruck. He didn't waste any time establishing a relationship with Anna, and his horse got quite a workout traversing between Apia and Lufilufi as often as his owner could possibly go.

Anna told Fritz everything about her relationship with Jamerson, but this confession didn't dampen his enthusiasm; somehow, on the contrary, it enflamed it. They planned a marriage

CHAPTER 18

in the summer and applied for the required licenses at the local courthouse who then pasted the applicant's names and dates of marriage on the bulletin board adjoining the courthouse door. They decided to list the twenty-fifth of August as their wedding date but secretly married on the ninth, just in case Jamerson would show up and wreck the ceremony.

Their plan was effective because on the twenty-fourth Jamerson turned up at Anna's house, the one he built, and called her out. He was drunk and had a pistol in his hand and was in no mood for talking. Unfortunately, von Reiche wasn't home at this time and the Samoan girls who worked for Anna came running in, screaming that Jamerson was there with a gun. She gathered up her bravest face and went out to meet him. She talked to him on the balcony and told him he was too late: she was already married and he might as well leave. Willie was so distraught he fired the pistol in the air and dismounted; he stormed up the stairs and banged on Anna's bedroom door. The door was locked and barred, and Anna and her girls were hidden under the four-poster bed. Willie, in a drunken rage, shot the pistol through the bedroom door and promptly left.

Jamerson, as a last resort, took Anna to court suing her for the work he did for her on the schooner, house, and buggy he built. The court date arrived and he thought it would be an open and shut case, but Anna was a better businesswoman than he gave her credit for. She produced every receipt for the materials and labor he required of her. He didn't charge her very much for his work, hoping to collect the rewards later on in their relationship. When he complained to the judge regarding his poultry profit, he was asked whether the money paid was what he asked for. He had to reply in the affirmative and then had to suffer the sting of losing.

It was determined that he was duly paid for work rendered and the case was thrown out of court.

The wedding day came and even though the ceremony was private they had plenty of guests and all went off without a hitch. The celebration was enjoyed by the whole village and the gifts were plentiful and varied. The Samoans gave Anna gifts befitting her rank in the village hierarchy but seemed trivial to Fritz. The most prestigious gifts that Samoans can give are their beautiful mats; the finer the weave the more valuable the mat. To Fritz, it was just another mat but to Anna, it was a special honor and she treasured the sacrifice the natives so willingly bestowed upon her this day. She had several mats and the one most precious was called "Made With Spectacles".

Later on in their marriage Fritz was complaining that he wanted a new carriage and couldn't afford one right then. Anna called the chiefs together and struck a deal. The next day a brand new carriage appeared with two white horses and all the tack to complete the set. Fritz came to the house and inquired as to the owner of the carriage. Anna said, "It's yours."

"What?" he said.

"Yes," she went on to say, "those old mats you were laughing at, that we got for our wedding; well, I traded the worst one of the bunch to a neighboring chief and got this carriage for you." He never took anything for granted after that experience and had a healthy respect for the Samoans and their ways.

The ceremony and "fiafia" was over and the newlyweds headed off for their honeymoon. Fritz took Anna aside and with all seriousness tried to make a point. He stated once again that as far as he was concerned, all previous actions were forgiven and he

CHAPTER 18

would never bring them up again; that he wanted to start their relationship fresh and with no excess baggage. Anna was oblivious to his accusations but smiled and went to ready herself for their first night together. She still smiles as she relates this part of the story. She said later on that evening that all Fritz had to say with humble admiration was, "Poor Willie, Poor Willie."

CHAPTER 19

Gorbachov was instigating his new society in Russia and the requirements for entry lessened. All that was needed was a letter of interest from a Russian company inviting you to Russia for a visit to do business, and you were in. The Berlin wall came crashing down during this time and even though perestroika was emerging, it was still very "iffy" to travel there. I had no intentions of going to Moscow, but after I had got a call from a friend of mine who expounded on this fantastic opportunity few Americans ever receive, I relented and decided to go. He had the letter, and all I needed to go was my passport, visa card and most of all a ticket from British Air Ways.

I had known Bill for years, and some of the antics he pulled were offbeat and incongruous. This either ticked off those around him, or worse yet, made them laugh. He had some wild idea of growing a hybrid crop of wheat that his close friend had developed. This friend and Bill were developing a strain of wheat at the University of Wyoming, just outside Casper, which had the same properties as marijuana but looked like wheat. They were going to make a killing growing wheat and selling pot right under the Feds' nose. They had invested years in this development and were nearing completion when something happened, and it all evaporated. I never found out what happened but either way, it fell through.

Another scheme he cooked up was stripping the military's nuclear silo's that were abandoned all over Wyoming of their precious metals such as aluminum and copper, and anything salvageable, and selling it for scrap. This was not a good idea and, thank goodness it had been conceived and failed before we met. Uncle Sam frowns on handing over his assets without a fight. While we were scrounging through a military scrap yard, Bill spotted a huge airplane wing tank used as a disposable drop tank that was jettisoned after the fuel was gone, usually over the ocean. It looked like a big torpedo with a tail fin. He was going to fix it up as a submerged tank that would be towed behind a fishing boat. He would fill it with marijuana and smuggle it across the border from Mexico to California. If the Coast Guard ever came sniffing around, he would just cut it loose and let it sink, then come back later and retrieve it. As I said, harebrained and weird were Bill's specialties.

I think the absolute worst idea he ever cooked up was his automobile insurance scam. It involved buying totally wrecked top-end cars, such as Cadillacs and Lincolns, and removing their tags. Then once he destroyed the car, he would rent an exact duplicate of the wrecked car, and after putting the tags on them he would drive to several insurance companies and sign up. He would then return the rental car and start making the monthly payments. He would keep up the payments for a couple of months and then one day, out of the blue, he would call the insurance companies and yell, "My car has been stolen." He finally got caught, maybe because insurance companies started interfacing with each other through this new media called computers. He was busted but not utterly destroyed, for people like Bill are never dissuaded from wrongdoing; they just can't conceive of doing anything legal for a living.

Bills greatest enemy was himself. He expected everyone to accept him just as he was which was more than rough around the edges. He was the poster child for the "People against Crack", and I don't mean the kind you smoke. His pants were seldom above his,

CHAPTER 19

and the show wasn't pleasant. He had no problem wearing checks and stripes combined which made me nauseous. He used to wash his clothes but never ironed them and this was before the wash and wear we have today. For him, wearing flip flops were acceptable in all situations and he would be comfortable wearing them to church or court, either one. I don't know why I would go different places with him at all. He was an interesting fellow and I felt the embarrassment was worth the benefit of witnessing whatever cockamamie stunt he would pull next, a decision I would regret later on.

I didn't know what this trip to Russia was all about but was assured there were no drugs involved. It was strictly on the up-and-up. Our plane left L.A. and after stopping at Heathrow airport in England, continued on to Moscow. I have a second sense that tells me whenever I put myself in harm's way or the possibility of such; it raises the hackles on the back of my neck and I break out in a cold sweat. Crossing the border into Mexico does it to me every time. It's as if I was a knight and I had to check in my armor just before a battle. You might say I felt nude in the Antarctic. Disembarking at Sheremetyevo Airport and walking down these dingy hallways through customs was ten times worse than Mexico. The customs agents must all have been battered children because none of them ever smiled or gave any indication of mirth or happiness. You could always pick out the Americans in the crowd because they were cracking up and happy and full of life, but these poor wretches were always miserable and distraught.

Moscow has some of the most beautiful subway systems in the world. There never was graffiti anywhere and the artwork at each stop was interesting to see. Nikita Khrushchev was the person responsible for the construction of the subway before his rise to power as the Party Leader. The mark of Communism was evident everywhere, especially in the Russian people themselves. Distrust and suspicion were stamped on each face as we traveled on buses or walked through shopping malls. People would watch us from the corner of their eyes but never full face; that would be rude. Many passengers on either the bus or subway would carry a book or novel and read as they traveled. I saw many more eyes watching us from above the pages than were reading their stories. We must have been a real sight to behold, utterly foreign to their method of thinking or reasoning, especially Bill.

We had a meeting to attend with Bill's Russian contacts, about five in all, and after we had settled in our hotel, we were met by them in our room. I can say that Russians are like any other European nation when it comes to business. They always wore a suit and tie and all the trimmings and put their best foot forward. Bill, on the other hand, looked like he escaped from Siberia, disheveled and unkempt. I had nothing to do with their meeting, but as an observer they always turned to me as if I was the one in command which ticked Bill off immensely. Bill, unbelievably, did have a high IQ but social graces he didn't have at all; zero, zip, nada. They were discussing the possibility of starting a limo service for all the "nouveau riche" popping up all over Moscow. Bill, with his vision of grandeur, wanted a villa in the middle of town with bodyguards, etc. I think he wanted to set up some kind of Godfather theme with him as Corleone himself. Just another Bill harebrained idea, except now he was exporting his insanity to foreign lands. I felt sorry for the poor Russians and made friends with some as the meetings progressed. They never actually stopped talking to me, but after I kept redirecting the conversation back to Bill they grew

CHAPTER 19

more agitated at his ridiculous demands. I could see the frustration on their faces, even if Bill couldn't. The only time I saw them happy was when Bill pulled a couple of thousand dollars out of his suitcase as an advance payment toward their joint venture. Bill was stupid in the handling of money, and with just a handshake he turned over to these strangers the equivalent of two years' wages for all of them.

I had to get away from the madness and took a walk to view some of the magnificent structures so prevalent in Moscow. There was snow on the ground. People were dressed in their furs and hats and the old "babushkas" (grandmothers) were lined up along the walkway holding some knitting or lace they had made to sell. They received such measly support from their government, many were literally starving to death and any income from whatever source was critical for their survival. They lined the streets in the snow and hustled for money. Little do we know how rough it is for others as we cash our social security checks and carp about the amount.

One poor soul was sitting on a bench outside a mosque praying with her head bowed and some sort of rosary beads in her hands. Nobody else was present and the weather had turned dark with the wind whipping up the loose snow on the seat beside her and on the ground. A more pitiful sight I had never witnessed and my heart went out to her. I slipped a few dollars into her freezing fingers and turned to leave. She jumped up from her seat and quickly grabbed my ankles, for she was kneeling in the snow in a shot and was trying to kiss my shoes. I was taken back and grabbed her by the shoulders and lifted her up and hugged her. She was crying and trying to tell me something in Russian I didn't understand. I think it was something to the effect that her prayers were answered. Two people left that place happy, one for giving and one for receiving, and I think that is the way it should be.

One friend I made during Bill's money-making frenzy was a man named Sergey Bondar. Sergey invited me to his home for a meal and I accepted. I left Bill with his new business partners and took a taxi to the address Sergey had given me. I picked up a bottle of vodka, available on every street corner for a dollar and arrived in time for dinner. The apartment complexes in Russia are all monotonously the same, square and symmetrical and cheap. The elevators don't usually work so I hoped it wasn't on the tenth floor where this dinner was waiting for me. The entrance to the complex stank of urine and due to the lack of public restrooms all over Moscow, it was no small wonder.

I made my way to the right apartment and knocked on the door. Sergey answered with his wife, all smiles and very hospitable, a stark contrast to the faces I witnessed all over town. He had a teenage son who met me with cautious reserve and never really warmed up to me the whole time. The meal was Spartan but tasty with slices of meat, cucumbers, and some other vegetables. We drank some vodka and visited for a while, which wasn't easy since Sergey spoke little English and I spoke no Russian. His son, however, spoke good English and was hospitable enough to translate for us. I spotted an old beat-up twelve string guitar hanging on the wall. When I say beat up I'm being kind; the finish was gone and it looked like raw wood with dirt smudges where the pick action would work. It had all the strings and I wondered if it was playable. I told Sergey, through his son, that I had a twelve string guitar at home. He plucked it off the wall and handed it to me to play. I shook my head and said, "You play." The vodka had taken effect and he tweaked the

CHAPTER 19

strings a bit to tune it before he played. To this day I marvel at the sound he managed to wring out of that pathetic instrument. It was marvelous. He played everything from Scott Joplin's theme from the movie "Sting", to more modern tunes from The Beetles to Burt Bacharach. He had a musical soul and played from the heart. His son told me he had a following in Russia for his renditions of their folk tunes, of which he played some for me. I had the presence of mind to ask if they had a tape recorder I could borrow to tape his playing. They produced a pink children's toy model, but it worked and I still have those beautiful tunes with me today. I play them once in a while but not too often for it brings back such bittersweet memories of Russia, Moscow, and Sergey Bondar.

It was time to leave and Bill and I packed up our stuff including lacquer boxes, military hats with insignias, military watches, and a slew of other souvenirs for our families.

Bill never made a cent out of Russia, but I did, as the people I met there wanted to do business with me. I sold many trinkets at the beginning when the dollar was worth thousands of rupees and the Americans hadn't yet screwed up the value of exchange. I purchased things from night-vision scopes to pilot helmets, which sold like hotcakes back home. Bill bought thousands of carabineers (a device used in mountain climbing) made of titanium which were a good deal at .15 cents apiece since they sell for $15 to $20 here in the States. He couldn't give them away because they weren't certified, and without certification you were open for endless litigation if someone got killed using them.

Another scheme had gone bad, which was becoming his "modus operandi". He had no one else but me to focus his frustrations on, and he took me to court to sue me for my success, saying that if it weren't for him I wouldn't have made a dime. I found out later the reason he took me with him to Russia was to act as an unknowing bodyguard; I imposed a foreboding presence at 6'2" and weighing in at the time 220 lbs. I should have known he wasn't capable of changing his stripes this late in life, and even though I did get a trip to Moscow, it didn't offset the stuff that came later.

I have pleasant memories of Russia and the people I met there, but Bill isn't one of them. He never won a penny from me and if I never see him again, it will be too soon.

CHAPTER 20

If I could just turn the clock back a few years, what a difference it would make in how things would be today. I remember once when Jim and I were exploring the ranch where he lived and also the surrounding areas, we came upon an old barn at the back of his neighbor's property. The roof was sagging and the sides collapsing and it hadn't been used for anything but storage for years. This is stuff dreams are made of and we were about to stumble on to a stash of items that was unique if not awe-inspiring.

The orange-ranching business is pretty much touch and go, especially with the changing weather conditions. The summer months are stable enough but during the colder times of the year, you have to be on your guard. If the temperature drops below freezing you had better be out there either lighting smudge pots or running the overhead fans to pull the warm air down to keep the crop from freezing and losing its value. If you have ever eaten an orange that has been frozen on the tree you will know what I mean; it is watery and tasteless, not worth eating at all.

Jim has set his share of smudge pots, and if he never sees another one, it will be fine with him. The smudge pot is a cylindrically-shaped device that has a reservoir at the base for diesel fuel and a chimney standing about five foot tall above it. You light the pot and it emanates enough heat to keep the fruit from freezing. They are placed between the trees about twenty feet apart and need to be refueled all through the night or until the temperature rises enough so you can extinguish them. The pots give off more than heat; they smoke terribly and after a night of tending them, you are covered with soot and look a mess. The overhead fans are electric and they look like big boxes on a derrick with a propeller attached on one end that enables the warmer air, that rises, to be rerouted back down and raise the temperature just enough to keep the fruit from becoming ruined.

Before the electric fans were available, the ranchers used aircraft engines to do the same thing. These were usually Pratt and Whitney radial engines used on fighter planes from World War II. They were cheap to buy back then and procuring a couple of dozen was no big deal. The cost of high-test fuel was not cost efficient and they were replaced years later by the more efficient electric ones.

The old barn Jim and I had happened upon was full of these Pratt and Whitney radial engines. They were stacked on the back wall and covered with an old tarp. There were about twenty of them and they were complete with all the pieces intact. I look back and shake my head because I know the old barn was torn down and the engines probably sold for scrap. This was back in 1963 and even then it was becoming more and harder to find parts for these antique aircraft. Today a Pratt and Whitney complete radial engine would bring close to a million dollars apiece. We were looking at a gold mine and if we could turn back the clock, as I said, things would be a lot different.

Another turn-back-the-clock story is also about ancient aircraft. I was working at a large medical center in East Los Angeles as the director of engineering and maintenance and I got to know many people who worked there. One of the staff and I became friends, his name was Dr. Bieler and his passion was old planes. Dr. Bieler was hunting for a restorable P51 Mustang and found one in the

CHAPTER 20

Mexican military somewhere south of the border. He went down there, bought it and flew it back to Long Beach where he began restoration. He said the trip home was a nightmare and he had to land it several times in fields and back roads to refill the oil tank as it leaked like a sieve and hadn't been maintained in years.

He completely tore the plane apart and rebuilt it from the ground up. He installed a new radio system in it as well as all the other amenities available at the time. The Mustang was outfitted with various engines but the best by far was the turbocharged Merlin Rolls and I think he had one installed in his P51. It took him several years to restore his plane and when it was completed, he had a magnificent flying machine most people only dream about.

I remember I was crossing the street between the maintenance department and the medical center and Dr. Bieler approached from the opposite side. He called me over to him and we swapped small talk for a while and then he said, "Wayne, do you want to buy my P51? I'm going through a divorce and I need to liquidate all my assets and I would like to sell you the P51 because I know how much you admire it. You can have it for thirty-five thousand bucks if you want it." I had just sold a house in Glendale and had the cash in the bank, but I was a new father with two kids to raise plus a wife who wouldn't understand the purchase of an airplane, especially since I couldn't even fly. I had to deny the generous offer and have rued the day ever since then. The P51 in the condition it was in would quickly bring several million today and as I mentioned before, if I could only turn back the clock, how different things would be now.

My sister, Maureen, worked as a personal secretary for the vice president of sales of a large toy manufacturer in Lawndale,

California. She was the one in the family we all figured had the brains of the outfit and could type faster than anyone I ever met. She was from the old school where you still had to learn to take shorthand, a talent long forgotten such as the use of the slide rule which was replaced with the calculator years ago. She attended a private college at La Sierra, California where the students could offset their tuition by working in various choices of the schools institutions. She got a job in the laundry so she could work the hours she wanted because the laundry worked around the clock. Most students just made some pocket money and didn't really put a dent in their tuition which most parents paid anyway. Maureen, when she quit, was owed money after her tuition was entirely paid for, and she managed an A average during her tenure there. It had never happened at the school before and when she withdrew was told so by the administration.

Maureen's boss called her into the office one day and she was told they were initiating a new line of dolls and asked would she like to get in on the ground floor by buying shares offered only to the employees. She wasn't familiar with the stock market or shares and was content with just a paycheck, so she declined. Her boss was the vice president of sales and periodically she worked for Ruth Handler, the owner of Mattel Toys, and the line of dolls was the Barbie Doll line. Like I said, if we could turn back the clock...

CHAPTER 21

I lived in Mount Albert, a little town just outside of Auckland, the largest city in the North Island of New Zealand. I lived with my maternal grandmother, my parents, my elder brother Rod, and three sisters, Maureen, Rita and Dulcie (chronologically listed). I was born in the Auckland hospital and went directly to my new home in Mount Albert and lived there for twelve years prior to moving to the United States in 1957.

I couldn't have asked for a more exciting place to grow up as a child. We lived on the farthest street from the main road and behind our house was a soccer field, and behind that was the city dump. The dump was in three parts. One part was for the household trash such as old food stuff and old clothes. Another was for old construction garbage such as wood remnants and wiring, shingles and all types of materials. Lastly, there was the commercial trash from businesses consisting of restaurant waste, small factory leftovers, etc. Behind the dump was a little creek that flowed year around and across the creek was the lunatic asylum, the worst one in New Zealand. It was an imposing sight on a hill, built of gray stone and reminiscent of the Shawshank Prison in the movies and surrounded by an enormous wall of wood. To the North of the "loony bin" was a rock quarry for the construction of gravel. It was now deserted, leaving an old train engine that had rolled off the track and lay on its side, rusting away over the years. South of the asylum and across the creek were some plum orchards and a huge greenhouse made of glass stained white from the calcium in the water hitting the window-panes year after year.

The neighborhood had many varied families and I had no lack of friends. The Mitchel boys were my closest friends, Ian and Trevor with their little Sydney Silky dog named Tinker. Ian was the same age as me and Trevor was a couple of years older. Wayne Hillman lived catty-corner from my house since we lived on a T-intersection, and the Windsor kids, Mavis, and her sister, lived further up the hill. Mavis was very athletic and could outrun all of us, but she had a unique disability that we all accepted though never understood. It was just a way of life for all of us and Mavis suffered the consequences. She had a way of stopping whatever she was doing at the time and pass out on her feet. Her eyes would roll back in her head, and she was out cold for a few seconds and then come out of it and she would carry on as if nothing ever happened. I don't know the medical term for this anomaly, but it caused many hilarious episodes. These occurrences happened several times a day and, of course, there was no warning as to when they would happen.

We were all poor kids, but we never realized it as we grew up together. Distinctions between rich and poor were nonexistent with us kids; we just accepted each other as equals. We would roam between each other's homes and treated as family by all. It was an ideal situation, and none of us ever suffered from a lack of love and concern.

My mother had an old German ritual of putting bread in the oven to dry out when it became a little stale. The pilot in the oven was enough to do the job, and all of my friends used to come over for the "hard bread" she made. We called it "Zwieback" because that is what our grandmother called it. We didn't have all the amenities we have now, and I marvel at how my mom did such an excellent job

CHAPTER 21

of caring for us without them. We had no refrigerator, no washer or dryer, and no supermarket, but we did have indoor plumbing with hot and cold running water. Periodically we would have some chickens in the back yard for eating. Dad would bring them home in a crate, and it was Mom's job to cut their heads off and pluck them for dinner. I got a rudimentary education in hen anatomy with these essential slayings and dissections. It was interesting seeing the various stages of egg production as we eviscerated the hens in the kitchen sink. I was playing soldiers with Wayne Hillman in our back yard when one of these happenstances occurred. My Auntie Mina was visiting, and since she was a rough and tough woman like no other I ever met, then or since, she helped with the meal preparation. Wayne and I were in the tool shed roof overlooking the yard as Mina grabbed a likely candidate from the crate. We were discussing the attributes of battle and heroism and how we were going to be heroes and come home with medals for bravery and valor. The pots we had retrieved from the dump that served as helmets only added to the realism of the scenario. About that time Mina whacked the axe on the unfortunate victim and let it loose as it ran helter skelter around the yard, with no head, bumping into benches and shrubs until it finally stopped. Wayne and I looked at each other with wonderment in our eyes and I said, "That's going to be us if we go to war."

He said, "Yeah, I think I will be a train engineer instead."

It was a hot summer day, and we kids wanted some fun, so we decided to go paddling in the creek. The only problem was we had no canoe or paddles. We went to the local building supply, the dump, and gathered our construction materials. We found some corrugated tin from off a roof and some 2x4s and lugged them home. I said we need to jump on the tin to flatten it out, so we all joined in and did just that. We had two sheets nice and flat sans lumps and small irregularities. I cut the 2x4s to make the prow and stern of the canoes. This was no small task for ten-year-old kids. We then folded up the ends of the sheets, inserted the 2x4 pieces, and nailed the metal to them from both sides. Next we got into the canoe and spread the sides out and nailed a couple of 2x4 seats between the sides, thus forming a perfect canoe. There was just one small problem: the holes made from the nails when the sheets were nailed to the roofing trusses, and the ends where the 2x4s were installed needed plugging up. Luckily, not too far from our neighborhood, the city had just re-tarred a road and the tar on the edges where the rocks hadn't covered it was still soft enough to dig up and use as a calking for our new canoes. The paddles were no big deal, just a few pieces of wood with tin plates nailed to them served well. We hauled the canoes to the widest part of the creek and launched them. They floated perfectly, and each canoe held two kids. We waged war with each other and sank the enemy many times. Luckily the creek was shallow, and we all jumped in and hauled out the sunken vessels, tipped them over and re-launched them for further battle. It was incredible the fun we used to create for ourselves with the junk we liberated from the dump.

The public school system we attended was dark and dank just like the "Shawshank" behind our house. The buildings were made of stone, and the interior was mostly wood and stained dark like a scary movie set. I never liked school, and when my first-grade teacher grabbed me by the ear once for some small offense and

CHAPTER 21

practically lifted me off the floor with it, I was a devout school hater from then on. The government gave each kid a pint of milk and an apple every day and being a monitor, I was elected to take these goodies to the classrooms for distribution. If there were any leftovers, I got the bonus for myself. This was a good arrangement for me but seldom did there appear the hoped-for bonus since absenteeism was practically nonexistent in those days.

My sister, Dulcie (Dulc), who is four years older than me, had a track meet one afternoon, and her biggest contender was Mavis. We used to race each other at home, and it never failed; Dulc beat us all except for Mavis. The day of the meet was here, and the race set and ready to go. The kids were lined up, and the gun fired. They were off, and they had to run several laps around the soccer field. Out in front was Mavis and Dulc and it looked like a shooe-in for Mavis. They were approaching the finish line and then it happened. Mavis started slowing down and stopped. With one of her episodes, she froze and stared up into space and blinked a few times allowing Dulc to zoom past her and win the race out of pure luck and Mavis's malady.

Another colorful character living across town was Lester. He was a product of some significant damage to his brain, and his gait was affected with a little hop he interjected uncontrollably as he walked. He was given the nickname "Hoppy Les." because of this idiosyncrasy. He was an adult and feared by all the kids. When the alarm went out "Hoppy Les is coming", we all split in every direction as fast as our legs would move to avoid contact with him. These interruptions were mostly accepted with aplomb except when the event was compromised by some unforeseen incident. The alarm was given and the reaction predictable except for Mavis, who was doing her thing once again. She was out of it for a while and when she came to she was alone and face to face with "Hoppy Les". It was a good thing Mavis was a fast runner, and she showed us just how good she was that day as she did the 100-yard dash in about ten seconds flat.

Going into town was strictly forbidden without expressed permission from a parent. Using each other's bicycles was another no-no and punishable by a hiding or strap across the legs or worse. Dulc wanted to go into town for some free Eskimo Pies, given away by Santa Claus during a Christmas promotion by one of the local merchants. There was no way Dulc was going to miss out on a free Eskimo Pie, and she would tempt a fate worse than death for this coveted treat. Little did she know it would come close to that by day's end. She managed to talk Mavis into going with her. They took my older sister Maureen's bike and snuck off with it to town. Mavis sat on the handlebars, and Dulc pedaled from behind. This arrangement worked out well until Dulc got tired and said it was Mavis' turn to do some of the grunt work from the rear. They switched places, and Dulc should have known better than to let Mavis do the driving. It wasn't long before Mavis did her space cadet act and went flying down the street full speed with Dulc screaming from the handlebars and of course getting no reaction from Mavis for her frantic yelling. They hit the curb of the road going full blast that sent Dulc flying from her perch on the handlebars. Mavis went careening over the front wheel, with both of them ending up in the ditch banged up and bruised together. Dulc was giving Mavis hell to no avail because she was still out of it. When Mavis came round she did catch an ear full, but the damage was done. They sat there looking at the buckled front

CHAPTER 21

wheel with some of the spokes sticking out the sides, and some bent from the impact. The rim was bent, and there was no way this mishap would go unnoticed by the bike's owner.

They were pushing the crippled bike towards home when they observed a man working on his car in his driveway; they recognized him as the guy with the tin plate in his head from some accident or operation. He was also as feared as "Hoppy Les", but not as profoundly, so Dulc, ever the one for original thought, figured she would ask him to help in this hour of need. She and Mavis pushed the bike to the stranger. When she asked him if he could straighten the rim a bit so they could ride the bike home, he took his wrench and pounded the remaining spokes even worse than before. An act of meanness reinforcing the reason he was feared in the first place. This was the last straw for poor Dulc, and the journey home was only made worse by Mavis having another fit, driving the inevitable point home that she was really in for it.

In America, the kids our age were equipped with their weapon of choice called a slingshot. In New Zealand, we had the counterpart called a "shanghai". I don't know where the name came from, but just the sound of it conjures up many colorful incidences when we used them. The Shanghai is simply a strip of rubber usually cut from a car tire inner-tube about an inch wide and about sixteen inches long. The pouch was usually a tongue of an old shoe cut out and punctured on either side with a hole for a string to be threaded through and tied. This created a loop of string about eight inches from ear to ear. The loop was fastened into a slip knot and wrapped around one of the ends of the piece of rubber. A stone, or on special occasions for accuracy, a marble, was inserted into the pouch and gripped from the outside of the pouch and pulled back with the right hand while the left hand held the other end of the rubber strip. You aimed it by sighting down your arm and letting the pouch go when sighted inappropriately. These weapons were archaically efficient and with a little skill could be used to hurl a stone quite a long way with mediocre accuracy.

The favorite hunting site was the garbage dump where all the rats were, plus seagulls by the hundreds. We never shot at the gulls, but the rats were fair game. They were a wary prey, and it took a lot of patience on our part to wait for them to come out to feed before we let loose. We would hit one sometimes, and this was always an opportunity to crow about out prowess.

Another weapon we sometimes made was an "abo arrow". This was an arrow made from a straight piece of a branch about two feet long and about a half to three-quarters of an inch in width. At one end, we would sharpen it to a point and the other end we would split two ways crosswise from each other. These allowed a slot for fins to be installed. These fins were fashioned from an old cereal box, cut in the shape of a heart by folding the cardboard in two and cutting half a heart and when you opened it up you had two fins which you slipped into these slots. The end was tied shut when you had installed the fins and then a notch was carved around the shaft just below the fins. You got a long cord about two feet, six inches long and tied a large knot in one end. Holding the knot in the notch, you wound the string around the shaft, looped it over the knot and strung it down the arrow shaft to the pointed end. By holding the string taught and with the free end wrapped around your fingers that held the arrow, you could throw it easily the length of a football field where it stuck in the ground beyond the

CHAPTER 21

goal posts. I was the only kid that used the abo arrow and I usually threw it alone because I didn't want to pin any of my friends to the goal zone at the far end of the field. I thought about getting a patent on this home-made toy in later years, but the lawsuits from maimed and mangled kid's parents made this venture a total bust.

The reason they called the people in the asylum "lunatics" is because the phases of the moon has an effect on them. I know this from personal experience. The asylum was a good mile from our house and on cold wintery nights, on the full of the moon, these men would raise such a ruckus it would raise the hair on the back of your neck. The screaming and yelling and banging of objects against the steel bars were easily heard from our home in the suburbs. What made the scene even worse was when they had an escape they would sound the siren, and that was enough to scare the hell out of the bravest souls. When this happened, we were supposed to shut our windows and lock our doors until we got the all clear. One time they had an escape, and they found the guy a few doors down from our house sleeping in a neighbor's laundry room behind their back door. This was scary stuff, and we took any such occurrences with absolute seriousness.

The worst inmates were housed in this facility, and that meant the criminally insane, murderers, rapists and the dregs of society. My sister Maureen (Maur) was the best scary story teller there was. She had the ability to get you so scared you would rather pee the bed than risk an encounter with some maniac between your bedroom and the toilet two doors down. She got in trouble many times from frightening us younger kids half to death with her unusual talent. It never failed, and if my cousins visited with an overnight stay, we always begged Maur for a scary story. On one such occasion, we were huddled around the fireplace while Maur waxed eloquent with her spine-tingling forte. About then my mom told Rita, my middle sister, to go out to the back porch and fetch some coal for the fireplace. She protested but to no avail, it was her turn, so she gingerly crept to the coal bin at the back of our house in the dark. My dad, who was just then arriving from work, happened around the corner of the house and appropriately said, "Boo." I don't think Rita hit the ground from the coal bin to the fireplace, and her screams could be heard by the loonies for a change. I know she wet her pants, and Dad caught hell from Mom for frightening the kid half to death. I could never figure out why it was never more than "half" to death. Because I was sure Rita was closer to "all to death" than just "half". Poor dad was just in the right place at the right time and his timing, "right on queue", with the mood set by the master storyteller, Maureen…

CHAPTER 22

Parry Ray was a close buddy of mine during the middle sixties and early seventies. He was a devout surfer and used to lug his surfboard around in a beat-up Chevy van. The van was our only mode of transportation, along the coast cities of Redondo Beach, Manhattan Beach, Hermosa Beach and others in Southern California. He had an old mattress tossed in the back for extended stays at whatever place he happened to end up. It was a great arrangement, especially if he was able to entice a girl to share this meager arrangement, which was more often than not.

He worked at a gas station at a time when pumping gas and checking tires for customers was expected rather than the self-serve we use today. This was a golden opportunity for him to pick up gals on the loose, and even though he wasn't the most handsome dude in town, he had a way about him that served his purposes well. He didn't kiss the Blarney stone, he ate it whole. I could never believe the absolute crap he doled out to these gullible women who eagerly swallowed everything he said with apparent enthusiasm. Many times I had to turn away to keep from bursting out laughing at his ridiculous line of flattery which somehow worked. The guys that hung out with him, as well as myself, unanimously agreed that he should have been a stand-up comic because he had the ability to keep us in stitches whenever he had the notion to. He wasn't particular about his prey's looks or size; as long as they were female and between the ages of sixteen and sixty, he was ready and willing.

Parry had two cousins attending Fresno State University on an agriculture scholarship. They were Leon and Benny Jennings, both rough and tough cowboys in every way since they were raised on a ranch just outside of town. They played football and had wild parties on the weekends which we felt needed our attendance periodically. The drive up to Fresno took about four hours so it wasn't a long journey, but it required an overnight stay somewhere.

Leon lived in an apartment complex with a pool which was ideal for outrageous parties and carrying-ons. There was also an aunt, Noreen, who lived in a little community outside of Fresno called Riverdale with her husband, Dale, and several kids. She was the hearty homestead type of woman that took no BS but had a heart of pure gold and a husband that would give you the shirt off his back if necessary, even if it was his only one. This would be our home-base while we were in town so we dropped off our sleeping bags and other stuff and headed back to Fresno for some fun. We arrived a little early at the apartment and Leon was getting ready to drive to some guy's place to retrieve a debt owed him for some time now and he invited us to tag along, which we did. We didn't know what we were getting into as we rumbled down the dirt track to the man's front gate. We all piled out of the pickup truck and stood at the wooden gate about fifty feet from the man's front door. He was sitting on his front porch with a large pit bull dog by his side.

As I said before, Leon was not someone I would want to mess with. He stood about six foot three and had shoulders on him as wide as an axe handle. He wore western wear and always cowboy boots and hat when applicable. The man knew why we were there and his smug grin showed us he wasn't worried as long as his trusty dog was close at hand. Leon said he was there for his money and that he was coming in to get it. The man said if he set one foot in his yard he would sic his dog on him, and don't think he

CHAPTER 22

wouldn't. Without a split second to think it over, Leon opened the gate and walked in and then the man did sic his pit bull on him. Parry and I stood there transfixed with our mouths slack and our eyes wide open in disbelief. The dog came at Leon at a full run and just when he sprang for Leon's throat he was met with a swift and powerful kick to his abdomen by Leon's pointed toe boot, that felled the dog in one foul swoop. Leon, without breaking stride, approached the man on the porch who was by then heading into his house, screaming that he would get the money and be right out. After paying his debt with shaking hands and ashen face, he retreated back into his hole, leaving his trusty body guard lying unattended on the front lawn. We loaded back into the truck and left as quickly and unobtrusive as we had come.

It was Friday evening and the party was just starting to warm up. The girls from the university were arriving and the keg was tapped. Parry was already cracking jokes and the festive mood was beginning to bloom. It was a wild and crazy night, as Steve Martin would succinctly put it. By midnight, the empty kegs were floating in the pool and the revelers were jumping off the apartment roof into the deep end, some clad and others only half. By now both Parry and I were three sheets to the wind ourselves, and his laconic one-liners and astute impressions of various celebrities had everyone splitting a gut from laughing so much.

Marsha was one of the regulars who had a crush on Leon. She had made the mistake of telling one of her girlfriends that when she laughs real hard, she can't control her bladder and inadvertently leaks a bit from the stress. Naturally this piece of news lifted the bar of achievement and Parry was up for the challenge. I couldn't bear to see the poor victim laid waste by the murderous attack and had to withdraw. By two o'clock I was pretty much done in so I found the van and crawled in the back to crash for the night, leaving Parry and the gang to continue 'till early dawn.

Noreen had called the apartment and invited us to Riverdale for a BBQ at her place, telling us that her husband, Dale, had killed a sheep the prior evening and was butchering it up for us that afternoon. I dearly love roast mutton and heartily agreed, so we drove out there as soon as we had some Alka-Seltzer to calm the tummy first. The dinner was delicious and the weather perfect. As we sat in the back yard, I dug the guitar from out of the van and entertained the kids with some sing songs and a little pickin' and a grinnin'. Noreen enjoyed the time spent with the family and I still feel the wonderful sense of wholeness and unity as we all joined in with the homespun entertainment of an old guitar and some old-time songs from earlier days and forgotten times. We swapped stories till the sun went down and the beer ran out, then we each dragged ourselves into the house and crashed till morning.

Dale shook me awake at five am and said he was hauling a truckload of sheep to Hanford and would I like to ride shotgun with him. I said, "Sure", dressed quickly and we went outside to the waiting rig. It was a double-decker semi-truck made from aluminum and capable of hauling a hundred or more sheep at a time. He kicked it into gear and we hit the road for the loading dock where the shipment was waiting for us. It only took a few minutes to load the trailer and from the looks of some of the sheep, they were ready to drop their lambs at any time.

The trip to Hanford wasn't far and as we neared the fenced area where we were to drop them off I spotted the shepherd and his dog waiting for us there. He was a Basque by birth and his manner of

CHAPTER 22

speaking was difficult to understand, but he was very hospitable. After the sheep had been unloaded and the new mothers attended to, he motioned us toward his small trailer for something to eat. I was hungry by then and thirsty too from the revealing of the night before. His trailer was tiny and looked like the teardrop type made in the early twenties or thirties. The interior was cluttered with sausages hanging from the ceiling and wine bottles stacked in the rack towards the front wall. He pointed to some seats around a small table that was dropped down from the side wall and was propped up by one leg at the table edge. He retreated to the paddock in front of the trailer where he dug up a Dutch oven that had been simmering there for some time. At the trailer door, he popped the lid and the most beautiful loaf of bread was inside, golden brown and smelling like heaven. A quick wipe of the table and the loaf was there with some homemade salami and homemade wine. He procured some glasses and a sharp knife, and hacked off a huge slab of salami for each of us as well as some bread and filled the glasses with wine. This was a meal of real ambrosia fit for the gods of Greece or Rome and welcomed with much enthusiasm and appreciation. I will never forget that simple meal shared with a Basque shepherd who barely spoke English but had the gift of genuine hospitality.

We left the shepherd and his dog there and drove the rig back to Riverdale and the waiting family to once again renew the fun and games we had so heartily enjoyed the day before.

A few years before this event I had attended a camp meeting in Lynnwood California where I met a beautiful girl named Trinette. It was an unusual name and I have never come across it since. She was several years older than me, but we got along fine and had a lot of fun there in the summer heat. Towards the end of camp meeting time, she started to feel ill and needed to lay down for a rest in her parent's tent that they had rented for the occasion. The tents were lined up in neat rows and each had a light and an outlet for hair dryers and shavers and such. She started to feel worse and wanted to go to the medical facility so I helped her up and we started for the nurses' station. We hadn't gone far when she felt real sick and we ducked between the tents where she lost her last meal. I held her head and made her as comfortable as I could. She rallied a bit and felt good enough to return to the tent and rest. By the next day, she was fine but unfortunately camp was over and she returned home with her family. We corresponded for some time but lived too far apart for a lasting relationship. The last thing I heard she had graduated nursing school and had moved north, to Fresno, with a new husband.

With all the repartee at the ranch, I still felt a little lonesome since I was the one and only stag at the time. I remembered Trinette and decided to call the surrounding hospitals for a nurse named Trinette. I had no idea what her new last name was but figured her first name should suffice. It was the second hospital I called that I struck pay dirt and found a Trinette who was the head surgical nurse on duty that very hour. The operator put me through and I heard Trinette for the first time in many years. When I said who I was, she screamed into the phone and wanted me to come over and see her right away. It was second shift and late already, but I told Parry I wanted to go and see her. He understood and let me drive the old van to the hospital to see my old friend. She was on the top floor and when I got out of the elevator I could see someone down the hall in green scrubs and the little booties and shower

CHAPTER 22

cap thingy on her head. She spotted me, came running down the hallway, jumped up on me and wrapped her legs around my waist, and gave me the biggest kiss I had needed for many moons. I stood there stunned but grateful as she unlocked her legs and slowly slid off me but not releasing me by any means. She looked beautiful even with the get-up on, and she still had the sparkle in her eyes I cherished many years ago. She kissed me again and said, "Hi, good lookin'. You're a sight for sore eyes!" She said she only had a little time before she got off and for me to wait for her then we could go to her place and talk. She had been divorced for a couple of years and was living with her large German shepherd dog for company and protection.

I called Noreen and said I was staying with a friend for the evening and would meet up with them tomorrow. She wanted to know where I would be so I gave her the address and phone number of Trinette's apartment. That was a fatal mistake. The night I spent with Trinette was fantastic and catching up on our lives was enjoyable. She told me about her marriage and subsequent divorce and the abuse she endured for too long from a man she thought she knew. She remembered the kindness I had shown her when she was sick and heaving, and said that most men would have left her standing there alone and suffering, ambivalent of her needs at the time. It's amazing how a little kindness goes a long way and how it is remembered for many years. Our time together vanished into the night and the early morning sun aroused us prematurely but emphatically to another day.

The horn was blaring in the driveway before my eyes were fully open and Parry and Leon, as well as some other kids, were yelling for me to come out because Noreen and Dale had prepared breakfast for us all and we needed to go. I asked Trinette if she would like to come, but she had an early shift to work and couldn't go. I foolishly dressed and left her there as we shot into Riverdale for breakfast. She never really forgave me for that rash decision and when it came time for Parry and me to leave that afternoon, she was at work and we never saw each other again. I regret bitterly the outcome of that meeting and if I could reset the clock of time I would happily do it differently, but being young and immature in many ways I fouled that up beyond repair. I often think of Trinette and wonder how she is doing, and even though it was two wives and three kids ago, I still have fond memories of the beautiful woman with the special name, Trinette.

Parry enlisted in the army soon after our trip to Fresno and soon found he was heading for Vietnam. After a brief stint at some fort for basic training, he was on a means of transport to the war. He wrote me several letters about how screwed up everything was there and of course I couldn't help laughing at his way of looking at things. His twisted sense of humor was still evident in his colorful descriptions of life in the army. Over a period of time, the humor became less and the sarcasm more. He came close to death many times and a lot of his close buddies were blown up in front of him or fatally shot in some way or another. He was a medic and so he landed right in the middle of the worst fighting and had to respond to the yell, "Medic, medic." He wrote me and said a lot of times that he didn't want to answer when the bullets were exceptionally hot and furious. He knew if he didn't though he was opening himself up to be "accidently shot" by friendly fire. He knew of more than one medic getting shot by his own men for cowardice. He said you have to look at it from the men's point of

CHAPTER 22

view, and if their medic refused to answer the call for help it might be them out there the next time and the coward could cause them their own life. He wrote to me about a lot of things that we never hear about in real life. Not only were the medics under scrutiny but the officers as well. Officers who were too gung ho and got their men into tight spots were subject to a stray bullet also. He earned some rest and recuperation at a base further behind the lines and was looking forward to the time spent there. He was utterly disappointed when he arrived and was consequently mugged by some unscrupulous gamblers and dope heads and couldn't wait to go back to the fighting for the rest.

He managed to survive Vietnam, and he asked me to pick him up from the airport in Los Angeles when he arrived. I did, and we hugged and yelled and jumped around a bit to let off steam. We loaded up his gear and started for his home. He said he wanted some good American chow for a change and to stop at a restaurant so he could get a hamburger and fries. We found a Denny's and I pulled in and we went inside and found a booth at the back. We ordered our food and while we waited, a truck drove by the front door and backfired. I looked over to see what caused the noise and when I looked back, Parry was gone. I looked around and about then he came crawling out from under the table. He was in uniform and it looked strange, him on the floor on all fours in a restaurant with sweat on his brow and visibly shaken from the noise. He sheepishly crawled back into his seat and said in a low voice, "Some things you do on instinct or you're dead, and you can't just shut it off like a switch." The people in the restaurant thought it was funny. I was incensed at their callous attitude toward a soldier who was fighting for their government and risking his life for their sorry asses and this ridicule was his thanks. The vets from Vietnam really got the short end of the stick in so many ways. It was a shameful time for the American public and some of the prominent figures who encouraged the stigma. Parry and I never talk anymore and his wife said he drives around crying for no apparent reason and it is driving him crazy. He is definitely suffering from post-traumatic shock, the effects of Vietnam, but that doesn't help him here and now, and I wish he had never gone. I haven't talked to him for many years. The last time I did, he politely asked me to never contact him again and I have acquiesced to this request. I will never forget the precious memories I treasure from this once wonderful, unique, and humorous friend I loved.

CHAPTER 23

His name was Arnaldo Ramirez Villapudua, but everyone just called him Primo. He worked at the hospital where I worked and was known for his ability to do almost any construction trade from cement work to installing dropped ceilings and to do them well. He was a man to reckon with, someone who didn't take any guff and didn't dole it out either. He just wanted to be left alone and tried his best to stay in the background and melt in with the scenery. He wasn't tall, or especially stout, or in any other way stood out from the norm, but his demeanor just cried out to troublemakers that he was cocked and ready if they wanted trouble. He had some boxing history and was capable of taking care of himself in most circumstances. He carried some scars from previous encounters and living in East Los Angeles, he was already halfway to trouble anytime.

Primo liked to drive black Ford pickups with chrome roll bars and off-road lights lined along the top of them. Chrome wheels and a hot engine was a necessity; the glass packs that growled oh so sweetly added to their wild personas. He went through several pickups over the years that we were friends and he prided himself on the wheels he drove. He had a "Rancho" in Sinaloa, Mexico that he never tired of describing, and there was a standing invitation for me to go there with him whenever he managed a trip, usually once a year. He had a wife and family there, and he sent money to them regularly for their support. He also had a wife and family in Los Angeles. He explained to me the way things were in the Mexican society, and as long as he was a good provider to his families and wives he was doing his part and everyone was happy. I didn't know how happy his wives were but it seemed to be working for the many years we were friends.

He had a cousin in Mexico he wanted me to meet, who was an accomplished lawyer. He said she had the most beautiful green eyes and auburn hair. With the curvy wave of his hands, he instilled in my mind a curvaceous body that along with a wink and smack of his lips, had to be outlining Venus herself. I am a sucker for brunettes and with the Mexican beauties I have seen I could only guess at the extent of his enthusiasm in selling his cousin. I was already happily married so I declined his offers at joining his way of life, a step I couldn't even conceive of, let alone partake of. He did manage to take a young man with him who was a co-worker at the medical center we all attended, whose name was Rodney Turner. Rodney worked as a maintenance man and was around twenty-one or two at the time. He was blond and good looking and had no trouble with girlfriends. When he went with Primo to Sinaloa, he went with the idea of having a good time and maybe finding a girlfriend or two there as well.

I guess Primo wasn't exaggerating when relaying information regarding his cousin; Rodney came back from his visit entirely infatuated with this siren. He was a pre-med student and no slouch in the intelligence department and this lawyer was every bit a match for him. He flipped over her lock, stock, and barrel. She was, of course, a lot older than he, but that didn't matter to him; he was smitten, big time. I'm glad I never went myself because even though my marriage eventually took a tumble, I didn't want to be the cause of it, and from Rodney's reaction I might have been.

It was late one night when I got a collect call from an Arnaldo

CHAPTER 23

Ramirez, from the Los Angeles jail where he was taken after a fight in a local restaurant. He had taken a date there (oh, I forgot to mention that he had several girlfriends as well as his two wives), and was challenged by a patron who thought the girl was more his than Primo's. The guy had a knife and was not hesitant about using it on his opponent. Primo grabbed a fork off the nearest table and shoved it into the man's cheek just under his right eye. The fight was over and the police were called along with an ambulance for the bully who started the whole thing. The man eventually lost his eye. They arrested Primo probably because he won the fight and I bailed him out the following day. I asked him why he stabbed the guy with a fork. He said all he could see was the other man's huge knife that he was preparing to carve him up with, and he wanted to stop it as soon as he possibly could. He did. The trial stretched out for years and I think Primo ended up paying the guy some money just to get it over with.

Guns have always been an interest to me and most of my friends. Primo was no exception. He had some of his own and the favorite we all liked was the Colt 1911 .45 Automatic. I had one and so did Jim, my friend of many years, who worked with us at the hospital on a contractual basis. Primo had the unique ability to cock the pistol by jerking it back with his one hand and causing the slide to disengage and cycle through a function, ejecting a round and loading another. This was a feat neither Jim nor I could ever match. Jim thought he would play a trick on him and he asked him to do it with his Colt Commander. The Colt was a much lighter pistol, and he also had a beefed up actuating spring, so the chances of Primo doing it was unlikely. Without a pause, he took the Commander and grabbing it with his right hand jerked it back and "bingo", cycled one through as slick as you please. I have never seen anyone ever do this feat since. It would be such a neat stunt to add to some movie sometimes as an attention getter. I can see all the guys in the "Hood" trying to emulate this feat with their Glocks, HKs, Berettas and other automatics.

Over the years, Primo succumbed to an affliction I am all too familiar with: Parkinson's disease. My mother, as well as a cousin, contracted this insidious malady that destroys your body from within as years creep by and you're helpless to counteract the symptoms. I had a doctor friend that was a prominent opponent of this dreaded disease. He found the area of the brain that controls the involuntary movements of Parkinson's patients and neutralizes it with electrical stimuli. He calls this procedure a "Pallidotomy". He performed this on my cousin and it was a remarkable improvement in the diseases symptoms. It wasn't an inexpensive process and cost my cousin $20,000.00 to have it done to him. Primo didn't have a bean, or should I say a chance, to get this done on himself. I talked with the doctor and he agreed to do it "gratis" as long as the medical center would do the same. He informed me later that week that they would, so we scheduled surgery ASAP. The doctor said I could attend the operation if I wanted to and that was an experience I didn't mean to pass up.

The day arrived and we all assembled in the basement of the hospital where the halo device was screwed to Primo's head. He had last minute x-rays and a cat scan and was finally wheeled to the operating theater on the upper floor. I scrubbed in with the doctor and put on my booties and shower cap and scrubs. The operating

CHAPTER 23

room was large with specialized equipment hanging from the ceiling and monitors lining the walls. Primo was transferred to the table and the halo inserted in a holding device that positioned his scalp right under the drill and probe that the doctor would use to do the pallidotomy. A one-inch hole was drilled into his skull and a long probe inserted to reach the offending pea-sized area that needed to be neutralized. Primo was awake during this whole procedure and was asked several questions by the doctor to follow the results of the inserted probe. Finally, the doctor asked if he saw any bright stars or lights and he said he did. The doctor turned to me and said he was getting close to the optic nerve and it was critical not to go too deep but also to be sure he went deep enough to get the job done. He asked Primo to raise his right arm, the worst one and keep it elevated while he zapped the "pea". Primo's arm was shaking, as usual, until the current was added and then his arm was still. We were all amazed at this sudden change, especially Primo.

The doctor said to his helper to close up and reinsert the plug of scalp removed earlier for access to the brain. The halo was removed and Primo sat up on the table with an incredible expression on his face. The doctor asked him to stand up and hold out his arms which he gladly did and there was no evidence of shaking at all, none. He then told Primo to walk down the hall, and after closing his gown at the back, he did. He turned around at the end of the hallway and literally ran back. He went from hobbling to running in such a short period of time. He hugged the doctor and thanked him profusely. I witnessed something that day I will never forget as long as I live.

Primo told me later that week the after-effects of this operation were unexpected but very much appreciated. His libido kicked into high gear and he said he felt like a teenager again. I don't think his wife was as excited as he was but nevertheless he was ecstatic.

I haven't seen Primo for many years, but I think of him often. One of his sons became a Los Angeles policeman; Raul, the one I named so many years earlier. I hope Primo is doing well, and if fate allows it, I will see him some time before we are beyond traveling or worse.

CHAPTER 24

Summer Camp. Two words that instill in most young people wonderment and excitement and the opportunity to act as raucously as possible since mommy and daddy were soon distant memories right after checking in. I was working at a well-known camp in the San Bernardino Mountains that had been in operation since the early fifties. It had grown from a few little cabins formed in a square around the lodge and mess hall to a conglomerate that would rival the Holiday Inn. My duties were very vague and could include everything from kitchen help to water ski instructor.

I had my bus driver's license so that duty was prominent in my work scheme. Being the bus driver had its pluses and minuses and even though it wasn't hard work, it had its moments. A typical Sunday would involve starting out from camp around eight am with a bus load of kids returning home. After dropping them off, load another bus full of excited kiddies and pack their stuff on the roof rack and head on back to camp. I was never assigned a helper to keep order on the bus and it got pretty dicey at times. With thirty to forty energetic seven and eight-year-olds while driving sixty-five miles an hour down the 10 freeway on Sunday afternoon in the middle of Los Angeles.

I managed to keep in one piece through the summer and it didn't get out of hand until the end of camp. The camp director thought it a good idea to have a couple of "special camps" for the underprivileged kids in the inner city area of Los Angeles, and maybe a camp for mentally challenged children. The latter we dubbed M.R. Camp, not to be politically incorrect, just telling it as it was. The first of the two camps was for the inner city kids. I arrived at the designated church where the "kids" were supposed to be waiting for the bus. As I approached the driveway, I saw hundreds of people standing around waiting but no children to be seen, anywhere. I drove to the center of the crowd and opened the bus door to get out and see what the situation was. I figured the kids were waiting in the building getting checked in or something and would soon be out to load up. Wrong! As soon as the bus door was open the crowd stormed the bus and started getting dibs on their chosen seats. I was literally slung back into my seat and just sat there while this mass onslaught transpired. The "kids" were six foot, to six foot six tall, and most weighed around 250 pounds plus. They were young for sure but give me a break, these guys were huge. I don't think the camp director thought this one through before opening up the doors to such a lot as these.

I didn't try to get control until after they had staked out their turf. After ten minutes of quieting them down, I said that their luggage needed to be loaded on the roof first before we were going anywhere. I assigned three of the biggest guys to help me out while the rest waited in the bus. I got on the roof and had the helpers throw the luggage and sleeping bags up to me so I could strap them down and get ready to leave. Some of the bags weighed around 100 pounds and the helpers chucked them up to me like they were throwing marshmallows at the circus clown. If I hadn't had a real foothold on the roof rack, the first bag would have knocked me clean off the roof to the other side of the bus.

We had a full load and the bus's capacity was 66 passengers. It was an old school bus and was powered by a V6 GMC engine. The engine put out a nominal amount of horsepower with a load of

CHAPTER 24

"school kids". It was not unlike a bus full of L.A. Rams linemen and heading for some of the steepest roads in California, or the whole nation for that matter. I wasn't going to be the one to tell these guys to get off, especially since some had literally climbed through the windows to get in. I told them that they all had to be sitting down before we started out and if they got up, I would stop the bus and not move again till they sat back down. I had them nod in agreement before we started and finally pulled out of the parking lot towards the freeway onramp.

They were just as excited as the little kids and I could tell they had never gone to camp before. It was enlightening to see the good this experience could be for them. It was a miracle they kept in their seats even though the noise was deafening at times. I happened to look out my rear-view mirrors and noticed the following traffic was at least one hundred yards behind me and this was in the middle of L.A. where the freeways were always clogged bumper to bumper. It wasn't long before I saw the reason for the huge gap behind me. I caught a flash of light as a bottle smashed onto the freeway behind me and then another, then more. I pulled off at the next off-ramp and stopped the bus. After the perfunctory moans and groans, I asked for all the empty pop bottles to be passed up to the front of the bus or we would be there for a long time. It wasn't long before we were on the road again.

The trip went pretty much uneventful until we pulled off the freeway and onto Highway 38 that led us to camp. This was the base of the mountain range and it was uphill all the way from here to camp. It was only a two-way road with a few passing lanes interspersed along the way. During the ascent, I had to drop the bus into granny low just to keep moving. I had up to twenty cars following me and blowing their horns until we reached the turnout up ahead and then I let them by. I almost handed out the empty bottles to the kids to hit the passing blowhards as they tore by and we resumed the slow trek up. Just before reaching the camp, there are a series of "S" curves on the highway prior to the decent into the camps parking lot. On these curves, the rear of the bus hangs over the rear axle by a long distance. It causes the back of the bus, the most coveted seats, to sway quite a lot as it traverses tight turns. The most trouble I had gotten on this trip was from this section and I thought a little revenge was in order. I was the only white person on the bus and the street slang was rife as we rode along, most of which I couldn't comprehend. I approached the "S" curves a little faster than I usually do and the whip in the back began in earnest as we hit the second "S". There were seven in all, and by the time I had reached the third "S" they were crying out for dear life. "Lordy, Lordy," was all too clear and, of course, the usual expletives that these kids knew all too well. I turned the ignition key off and on a few times as we descended in low gear. The low gear caused some enormous "backfires" and everyone ducked for cover as if we were in the middle of a drive-by shooting. By the time, we hit the last "S" it was quiet on the bus and we proceeded down the driveway in silence. I never saw so many "white-folk" get off the bus after that wild ride. I got a few, "You's a crazy man", and "Right on man", as they disembarked. I didn't much care what they called me, my job was done, I had gotten home in one piece and that was a "hellacious" fact.

 M.R. camp was a different ball of wax altogether. On this trip as I pulled into the driveway of the loading zone, I could see quite a few kids of all sorts and conditions. Some of the kids wore protective helmets and some were relying on aids to help them

CHAPTER 24

ambulate. My heart went out to them and I was invigorated as their excitement flowed over as they embarked for camp. There was about half a bus load and it was evident that they were in a different world than I lived in. I envied them, to some degree, as to their innocence and simplicity with which they faced life. I loaded their stuff and gave them the must-stay-in-their-seats speech and we were off. I watched some of the parents of these kids as I pulled out of the parking lot and I could see the relief on some of their faces and worry on the faces of others.

I hadn't gone more than a mile down the freeway before one of the kids started crying, and once one started, they all started in en-total. This wasn't a good start and I had another ninety-nine miles to go. I pulled off the freeway, went back to the kid who started crying first and gave her a hug. I sat by her and got her calmed down. The rest of the kids calmed down also, and after some hugs to the rest of them we were off once again. This scenario kept up for about every twenty miles, but I had no choice and did it with as much empathy as I could muster. The alternative would be a lot worse and I didn't want to come across as a big meany to kids who really didn't know what they were doing.

About the time, we reached Highway 38 the first request for the restroom popped up. Now I was in a quandary because I didn't want to lose control of the bus if we stopped. I escorted some of the kids into the restroom who apparently needed help in that department and leaving the rest on the bus unattended. I said we were only a few miles till we get there so hold on for a while and we could all go to the restroom then. It wasn't long before I caught the faint odor of an "accident" and it kind of spurned the rest into action and before long the smell was overwhelming. I had to brake for the next stop sign and a trickle of urine shot by my foot and puddled at the base of the gas pedal. It was quiet and I could only guess it was because they had done a "no-no" and were contemplating their fate for doing so. I tried to keep the swaying to a minimum as I traversed the curves and S-bends but to no avail; the first kid puked and then the rest followed suit. The smell of vomit and excrement was overpowering, and I too began to feel the need to puke. I held it down, but my eyes were watering pretty bad and my lunch kept threatening to reappear. I pulled up to a halt at the base of the descent and as the director approached, I opened the door of the bus and let him take in the full force of the moment. He reeled back as if hit with a baseball bat and I yelled out as he regained his composure, "I could have used some help on this run, boss."

We got the kids unloaded and cleaned up. I drove the bus to the garage, opened the back emergency door and took a fire hose from the rear to the front, floor, seats and all. The kids had a ball once they were cleaned up and assigned a counselor for every three or four children. I had all thirty of them by myself and that was a huge mistake in planning, not to mention I had to drive the bus as well.

As a parting shot, there was one last memorable trip I made just as the summer ended. I had to transport a black choir from East L.A. to camp for a retreat they were sponsoring as a morale booster and get-together. The choir consisted of many huge women as well as men who loved to sing and carry on as most people do when they are put together in a tight spot like in a bus. The bus was full and reminiscent of the inner city ride but without the bottle throwing and street jargon. The ride was kind of fun with song singing and constant cracks about this or that along with some

CHAPTER 24

comments about Rosa Parks and who would sit in the back of the bus. It was all done in fun and had us all cracking up along the way. There were about four or five women across the rear seat and they seemed to be the most vocal on all fronts. A more fun-loving group I hadn't seen in some time and the change was sound to behold. As we neared the S-bends, I couldn't help myself from, kind of accelerating a bit more than usual. The screams and shouts were sincere and from the depths of their well-rehearsed and developed diaphragms. "Oh, Lord God o' mercy", "Help us all now", "Heaven help us", and "Hallelujah" rang over the mountainside as we neared the camp entrance. I didn't have the heart to create some backfires on our descent and just kept a straight face as they all unloaded. The women from the back gave me a hug and said the E-ticket ride was invigorating and satisfying to the soul. I didn't get to carry them back to L.A. and was disappointed I wouldn't get the chance to enjoy their spirit and enjoyment of life once more.

AUTHOR'S BIOGRAPHY

I was born in Auckland New Zealand in 1946 right in the middle of the baby boom after WW II. I was raised in Mount Albert, a small suburb, at the time, just south of Auckland. Our small house was located a stones throw away from a soccer field which was surrounded by the city dump. What environment could be any more ideal for a kid to be raised in? There was Jock, the bulldozer driver, who lived in a shack behind our house, just over the fence, and his stack of girly magazines that helped us boys enter the age of enlightenment. He didn't appreciate us boys sneaking into his domain during his work day but he was a pretty good chum when it came to just hanging out there.

In 1957 we moved the whole family to the United States the whole family being my Mom and Dad, Maternal Grandmother Anna von Reiche followed in the order of age, my brother Rod then sister Maureen sister Rita and then the two "little ones" Dulcie and Wayne.

Life in the States was supreme and I loved every minute of it as we settled down in Torrance Calif. right next to Redondo Beach where the Beach Boys got their start at that time. I attended North High School, in Torrance for the first year then I went to

Newbury Park Academy in Newbury Park, Calif. for the remainder of my High School years. I attended La Sierra College in Calif. for a couple of years but never graduated.

I worked as a used car mechanic for Ray Vane Chrysler for a couple of years during the Road Runner episodes as well as the Challenger's, GTX's and the mighty Charger's I had more fun test driving these muscle cars after I tuned them up for resale. I could write a few chapters of these experiences alone. I worked for the Weesha Country Club for a couple years. As well as a stint of Logging in Roseburg, Oregon.

I worked for Hughes Aircraft on the "Surveyor space probe", and Northrup and Rockwell aerospace divisions on the B-1 and B-2 respectively. I retired in the late nineties.

I now reside in the Ozarks of Arkansas in a small town called Mountain Home where I will probably stay a while, awaiting the next chapter of Patchwork Memories.

www.ingramcontent.com/pod-product-compliance
Lightning Source LLC
LaVergne TN
LVHW051552070426
835507LV00021B/2544